Low-FODMAP Diet Cookbook

365 Days IBS Solution Recipes with 30-Day Meal Plan to Digestive Disorders and Soothe Your Gut

Georgina Miles

1

CONTENTS

Sauces, Dressings, And Staples 71

Desserts And Treats 77

Introduction

Hello everyone, my name is Georgina Miles, and I am a nutritionist and certified dietitian. Through my years of experience, I have helped many people manage their digestive issues and improve their overall health through a low-FODMAP diet. Today, I am excited to introduce my latest project, the "365 Days Recipes Low-FODMAP Diet Cookbook with 30-Day Meal Plan."

I wrote this cookbook to help people who struggle with digestive issues and need guidance in following a low-FODMAP diet. I noticed that many people who follow this diet often feel limited in their food choices or overwhelmed by the amount of meal planning and preparation required. That's why I wanted to create an all-in-one resource that provides easy-to-follow recipes, a comprehensive meal plan, and guidance on the low-FODMAP diet.

The "365 Days Recipes Low-FODMAP Diet Cookbook with 30-Day Meal Plan" offers a wide range of delicious, healthy, and easy-to-prepare recipes that are specifically designed for a low-FODMAP diet. This cookbook includes a 30-day meal plan, which takes the guesswork out of meal planning and ensures that you are following the low-FODMAP diet correctly. The recipes are organized by meal, making it easy to plan your weekly menu.

In addition to recipes, this cookbook also offers expert advice on the low-FODMAP diet, including tips for grocery shopping, meal planning, and dining out. This cookbook is designed to be a comprehensive guide to the low-FODMAP diet, making it easier for you to manage your digestive issues and improve your overall health.

Whether you are struggling with digestive issues or simply looking for healthy and delicious recipes, this cookbook has something for everyone. With expert advice, easy-to-follow recipes, and a comprehensive meal plan, this cookbook is the ultimate guide to the low-FODMAP diet. I hope this cookbook will help you achieve your health goals and live your best life.

What exactly are FODMAPs?

FODMAPs are a group of short-chain carbohydrates that are found in many foods. The term FODMAP stands for "Fermentable Oligosaccharides, Disaccharides, Monosaccharides, and Polyols". These carbohydrates are poorly absorbed in the small intestine, which can cause digestive issues in some people.

FODMAPs are found in a variety of foods, including fruits, vegetables, grains, dairy products, and sweeteners. Some examples of high-FODMAP foods include apples, pears, onions, garlic, wheat, milk, honey, and artificial sweeteners.

The reason why FODMAPs can cause digestive issues is that they are easily fermented by bacteria in the gut. This fermentation process produces gas, which can cause bloating, cramping, and other digestive symptoms. In addition, FODMAPs can also increase the amount of water in the intestines, which can cause diarrhea in some people.

For people who have digestive issues, a low-FODMAP diet may be recommended. This involves avoiding high-FODMAP foods and replacing them with low-FODMAP alternatives. The low-FODMAP diet has been shown to be effective in reducing symptoms in people with irritable bowel syndrome (IBS) and other digestive disorders.

It is important to note that not all people will experience digestive issues from FODMAPs. FODMAPs are a normal part of the diet, and many people can consume them without any issues. However, for those who do experience digestive issues, identifying and avoiding high-FODMAP foods can be an effective way to manage symptoms and improve quality of life.

How does the low FODMAP diet work?

The low FODMAP diet is a dietary approach that involves restricting the intake of fermentable carbohydrates to manage gastrointestinal symptoms in people with irritable bowel syndrome (IBS) and other digestive disorders.

The low FODMAP diet is typically done in three phases: the elimination phase, the reintroduction phase, and the maintenance phase. Here is an overview of each phase:

1.   Elimination Phase

During the elimination phase, high FODMAP foods are eliminated from the diet for a period of two to six weeks. This phase is intended to reduce gastrointestinal symptoms by removing the source of fermentable carbohydrates. During this phase, a dietitian or healthcare provider may provide guidance on which foods to avoid and which low FODMAP alternatives to include in the diet.

Foods that are generally restricted during the elimination phase include:

- Certain fruits and vegetables, such as apples, pears, onions, garlic, and mushrooms

- Dairy products that contain lactose, such as milk, yogurt, and cheese

- Certain grains, such as wheat and rye

- Sweeteners that contain high levels of fructose or polyols, such as honey, agave, and xylitol

During the elimination phase, it is important to monitor symptoms and keep a food diary to track which foods may be causing symptoms.

2.   Reintroduction Phase

After the elimination phase, the reintroduction phase begins, during which high FODMAP foods are gradually reintroduced into the diet to identify which foods trigger gastrointestinal symptoms. This phase typically lasts four to six weeks and involves reintroducing one high FODMAP food at a time, in small amounts.

During the reintroduction phase, a dietitian or healthcare provider may provide guidance on the amount and frequency of high FODMAP foods to reintroduce. After consuming a high FODMAP food, symptoms are monitored for a period of 24 to 48 hours to determine whether the food causes symptoms.

3.   Maintenance Phase

The maintenance phase involves developing a long-term eating plan that includes low FODMAP foods and occasionally includes small amounts of high FODMAP foods that do not cause symptoms. This phase is intended to maintain symptom control over the long term while providing as much dietary variety as possible.

During the maintenance phase, a dietitian or healthcare provider may provide guidance on which low FODMAP foods to include in the diet and how to balance nutrient intake. It is important to continue monitoring symptoms during this phase and adjust the diet as needed.

The low FODMAP diet is intended to help people with digestive disorders manage their symptoms by identifying and avoiding high FODMAP foods. By following this approach, many people with digestive disorders are able to improve their symptoms and achieve better quality of life.

What foods can you eat on a low FODMAP diet?

1. Proteins

Proteins are allowed on a low FODMAP diet and are an essential part of a healthy diet. Some low FODMAP protein sources include:

- Meat, such as beef, pork, and chicken

- Fish and seafood, such as salmon, tuna, and shrimp

- Eggs

- Tofu

- Tempeh

- Nuts, such as almonds, peanuts, and walnuts

- Seeds, such as chia seeds, pumpkin seeds, and sunflower seeds

2. Grains

Some grains are low in FODMAPs and can be included in a low FODMAP diet. Some low FODMAP grains include:

- Gluten-free grains, such as rice, quinoa, and corn

- Oats (in limited amounts)

- Spelt bread (in limited amounts)

- Sourdough bread (in limited amounts)

3. Fruits

Many fruits are high in FODMAPs and should be avoided during the elimination phase of the low FODMAP diet. However, some low FODMAP fruits can be included in the diet in small amounts, including:

- Bananas (unripe)

- Blueberries

- Cantaloupe

- Grapes

- Honeydew melon

- Kiwi

- Lemons

- Oranges

4. Vegetables

Many vegetables are high in FODMAPs and should be avoided during the elimination phase of the low FODMAP diet. However, some low FODMAP vegetables can be included in the diet, including:

- Carrots

- Green beans

- Lettuce

- Potatoes

- Spinach

- Tomatoes

5. **Dairy products**

Dairy products that contain lactose are high in FODMAPs and should be avoided during the elimination phase of the low FODMAP diet. However, some low FODMAP dairy products can be included in the diet, including:

- Lactose-free milk and yogurt

- Hard cheeses, such as cheddar, feta, and parmesan

- Butter

6. **Beverages**

Many beverages are high in FODMAPs and should be avoided during the elimination phase of the low FODMAP diet. However, some low FODMAP beverages can be included in the diet, including:

7. **Water**

8. **Tea** (except for black tea and chai tea)

9. **Coffee** (in limited amounts)

10. **Wine** (in limited amounts)

Benefits of a low FODMAP diet

1. **Reduces gastrointestinal symptoms**

One of the primary benefits of the low FODMAP diet is that it can reduce gastrointestinal symptoms in people with irritable bowel syndrome (IBS) and other digestive disorders. Studies have shown that the low FODMAP diet can reduce symptoms such as bloating, gas, abdominal pain, and diarrhea in many people with these conditions.

2. **Improves quality of life**

By reducing gastrointestinal symptoms, the low FODMAP diet can improve quality of life for people with digestive disorders. Many people with IBS and other digestive disorders experience significant discomfort and disruption to their daily lives due to their symptoms. By managing these symptoms with the low FODMAP diet, people can regain control over their lives and enjoy a better quality of life.

3. Increases dietary variety

Although the low FODMAP diet restricts the intake of certain carbohydrates, it also encourages the consumption of a wide variety of other foods. By focusing on low FODMAP foods, people can discover new foods and recipes that they may not have tried before. This can increase dietary variety and make meal planning more interesting and enjoyable.

4. May improve gut health

The low FODMAP diet has been shown to reduce the amount of fermentable carbohydrates in the gut, which can improve gut health in some people. By reducing the amount of fermentable carbohydrates, the low FODMAP diet may reduce inflammation in the gut and improve gut microbiota balance.

Breakfast And Brunch

Orange-vanilla Smoothie

Servings: 2
Cooking Time: X
Ingredients:

- 1½ cups orange yogurt
- ½ cup orange juice
- 1 orange, peeled and sliced
- ¼ cup vanilla-flavored whey protein
- 1 teaspoon vanilla
- 4 ice cubes

Directions:

1. Place yogurt, orange juice, orange, whey protein, and vanilla in blender or food processor; blend or process until smooth. Add ice cubes; blend or process until thick. Pour into glasses and serve immediately.

Nutrition Info:

- Info Per Serving: Calories: 346.91; Fat: 2.34 g ;Saturated fat: 1.22 gr;Sodium: 241.12 mg

Cinnamon Granola

Servings: 16
Cooking Time: X
Ingredients:

- 4 cups regular oats
- ¼ cup oat bran
- ¼ cup flaxseed
- 1 cup chopped walnuts
- ½ cup honey
- ¼ cup brown sugar
- 3 tablespoons orange juice
- ¼ cup canola oil
- ¼ teaspoon salt
- 1 tablespoon vanilla
- 1 tablespoon cinnamon
- 1 cup dried sweetened cranberries
- 1 cup raisins

Directions:

1. Preheat oven to 300ºF. Spray a cookie sheet with sides with nonstick cooking spray and set aside.
2. In large bowl, combine oats, oat bran, flaxseed, and walnuts and mix well. In small saucepan, combine honey, sugar, orange juice, canola oil, and salt and heat over low heat until warm. Remove from heat and add vanilla.
3. Pour honey mixture over oat mixture and mix well until oat mixture is coated. Spoon onto prepared cookie sheet and spread into an even layer.
4. Bake granola for 45 minutes, stirring every 10 minutes. Remove from oven, sprinkle with cinnamon, and stir in cranberries and raisins. Cool completely, then store in airtight container at room temperature.

Nutrition Info:

- Info Per Serving: Calories: 357.05; Fat:11.14 g ;Saturated fat:1.03g ;Sodium: 78.62 mg

Cranberry-cornmeal Muffins

Servings: 12
Cooking Time: X
Ingredients:

- ½ cup cornmeal
- ½ cup masa harina
- 1 cup all-purpose flour
- 2 tablespoons crushed flaxseed
- ¼ cup brown sugar
- 1 teaspoon baking powder
- 1 teaspoon baking soda
- 1 egg
- ¼ cup canola oil
- 1 cup buttermilk
- 1 teaspoon grated orange zest
- 2 tablespoons honey
- 1 teaspoon vanilla
- 1/3 cup chopped cranberries
- 1/3 cup dried cranberries

Directions:

1. Preheat oven to 400ºF. Line 12 muffin cups with paper liners and set aside. In large bowl, combine cornmeal, masa harina, flour, flaxseed, brown sugar, baking powder, and baking soda and mix well.
2. In small bowl, combine egg, oil, buttermilk, orange zest, honey, and vanilla, and beat to combine. Add to dry ingredients and stir just until moistened. Add chopped and dried cranberries.
3. Fill muffin cups full. Bake for 15–22 minutes or until toothpick inserted in center comes out clean. Let cool on wire racks for 10 minutes before serving.

Nutrition Info:

- Info Per Serving: Calories: 181.75; Fat:6.06g ;Saturated fat: 0.66 g;Sodium: 165.51 mg

Raisin-cinnamon Oatmeal Bread

Servings: 32
Cooking Time:
Ingredients:

- 2 (¼-ounce) packages active dry yeast
- ½ cup warm water
- 1¼ cups skim milk
- ¼ cup brown sugar
- ¼ cup honey

- 1 egg
- 2 egg whites
- 1/3 cup oat bran
- 1¼ cups oatmeal
- 3½ to 4½ cups all-purpose flour
- ½ teaspoon salt
- 2 teaspoons cinnamon
- 2 cups raisins
- 2 tablespoons butter, melted

Directions:

1. In large bowl, combine yeast and warm water; let stand for 10 minutes. In small saucepan, combine milk, brown sugar, and honey; heat over low heat until warm. Add to yeast along with egg and egg whites; beat until combined.

2. Add oat bran, oatmeal, and 1 cup all-purpose flour and beat for 1 minute. Let stand, covered, for 30 minutes. Then stir in salt, cinnamon, raisins, and enough all-purpose flour to form a stiff batter; beat for 2 minutes.

3. Spray two 9″ × 5″ loaf pans with nonstick cooking spray. Divide batter among the pans, smoothing the top. Cover and let rise for 45 minutes until batter is doubled.

4. Preheat oven to 375ºF. Bake bread for 30–40 minutes or until bread is firm and golden brown. Remove from pans, brush tops with melted butter, and let cool on wire racks.

Nutrition Info:

- Info Per Serving: Calories:138.98 ; Fat: 1.60 g ;Saturated fat:0.63 g ;Sodium: 54.50 mg

Dark-chocolate Orange Scones

Servings: 10
Cooking Time: X
Ingredients:

- 1¼ cups all-purpose flour
- 1 cup whole-wheat flour
- 1/3 cup brown sugar
- ¼ cup cocoa powder
- 1/8 teaspoon salt
- 1 teaspoon baking powder
- ½ teaspoon baking soda
- 5 tablespoons butter or plant sterol margarine
- 1 egg white
- ¼ cup orange juice
- ½ cup buttermilk
- 1 teaspoon vanilla
- 1 teaspoon grated orange zest
- 1 cup dark chocolate chips
- 2 tablespoons sanding sugar

Directions:

1. Preheat oven to 375ºF. Line a cookie sheet with parchment paper and set aside.

2. In large bowl, combine flour, whole-wheat flour, brown sugar, cocoa, salt, baking powder, and baking soda and mix well. Cut in the butter until particles are fine.

3. In small bowl, combine egg white, orange juice, buttermilk, vanilla, and orange zest and mix well. Pour over dry ingredients and stir until moistened. Fold in chocolate chips.

4. Gather dough into a ball and pat into a 9″ circle on the prepared cookie sheet. Cut into 10 wedges and separate slightly. Sprinkle with sanding sugar. Bake for 20–25 minutes or until scones are set.

Nutrition Info:

- Info Per Serving: Calories: 271.10; Fat:11.59 g ;Saturated fat:6.93 g;Sodium: 193.64 mg

Cornmeal Focaccia

Servings: 12
Cooking Time: X
Ingredients:

- 1½ to 2½ cups all-purpose flour
- 1 (¼-ounce) package instant-blend dry yeast
- 1 cup water
- 1 tablespoon honey
- 4 tablespoons olive oil, divided
- ½ teaspoon salt
- 1 tablespoon chopped fresh rosemary
- 2 teaspoons chopped fresh oregano leaves
- ½ cup cornmeal
- ½ cup masa harina (corn flour)
- 2 tablespoons cornmeal
- ¼ cup grated Romano or Cotija cheese

Directions:

1. In large bowl, combine 1 cup flour and yeast and mix well. In microwave-safe glass measuring cup, combine water, honey, 2 tablespoons olive oil, and salt. Microwave on 50-percent power for 1 minute or until mixture is very warm.

2. Add to flour mixture; beat for 2 minutes. Stir in rosemary, oregano, ½ cup cornmeal, and masa harina and beat for 1 minute.

3. Add enough remaining all-purpose flour to make a soft dough. Cover and let rise for 30 minutes.

4. Divide dough in half. Grease two 12″ round pizza pans with unsalted butter and sprinkle with 2 tablespoons cornmeal. Divide dough into two parts and press each part into prepared pans. Push your fingertips into the dough to make dimples. Drizzle remaining olive oil over the dough; sprinkle with cheese. Let stand for 20 minutes.

5. Preheat oven to 425ºF. Bake bread for 13–18 minutes or until deep golden brown. Cool on wire racks.

Nutrition Info:

- Info Per Serving: Calories: 182.86; Fat: 6.29 g ;Saturated fat:1.50 g;Sodium: 154.62 mg

Honey Rice Pudding

Servings: X
Cooking Time: 20 Minutes
Ingredients:

- ½ cup brown basmati rice
- 2 cups water
- 1 cup unsweetened nondairy milk (soy, almond, rice), plus extra for serving
- 1 teaspoon pure vanilla extract
- ⅛ teaspoon ground cinnamon
- Pinch sea salt
- ¼ cup dried unsweetened cranberries
- ¼ cup chopped pistachios
- 2 tablespoons honey

Directions:

1. Place the rice in a bowl and add the water. Soak overnight in the refrigerator, then drain.
2. Stir together the rice, water, milk, vanilla, cinnamon, and salt in a medium saucepan and place over medium heat.
3. Bring the mixture to a boil and then reduce the heat to low. Simmer until the rice is tender and the liquid is almost absorbed, stirring frequently, about 20 minutes.
4. Remove the saucepan from the heat and stir in the cranberries, pistachios, and honey. Add more nondairy milk if you like thinner pudding.
5. Serve.

Nutrition Info:

- Info Per Serving: Calories: 341; Fat: 8g ;Saturated fat: 0 g ;Sodium: 213 mg

Italian Baked Omelet

Servings: 2
Cooking Time: 20 Min
Ingredients:

- Cooking spray
- 6 large free-range egg whites
- ¼ cup unsweetened soy milk
- ½ tsp basil, chopped
- Himalayan pink salt
- Ground black pepper
- ¼ cup green beans, chopped
- ¼ cup red bell pepper, chopped
- ½ spring onion, chopped
- 2 tbsp. fat-free cheddar cheese, shredded

Directions:

1. Preheat the oven to 350°F gas mark 4. Grease 2 medium ramekins with cooking spray and set aside.
2. In a medium-sized mixing bowl, add the egg whites, soy milk, and basil, whisk until well blended. Season with salt and pepper, set aside.
3. Divide the green beans, red bell pepper, and spring onion between the 2 ramekins and pour in the egg white mixture. Top each ramekin with 1 tbsp. of cheddar cheese.

4. Bake for 15 to 20 minutes, until the baked omelet has puffed up and lightly browned. Serve hot.
Nutrition Info:

- Info Per Serving: Calories: 126 ; Fat: 4 g ;Saturated fat: 2 g ;Sodium: 164 mg

Whole-grain Pizza Crust

Servings: 12
Cooking Time: X
Ingredients:

- 1 cup warm water
- 2 (¼-ounce) packages active dry yeast
- ½ cup skim milk
- 2 tablespoons honey
- 2 tablespoons olive oil
- ½ teaspoon salt
- 1½ cups whole-wheat flour
- 1 cup cornmeal
- 1½ to 2½ cups bread flour

Directions:

1. In large bowl, combine water and yeast; let stand for 10 minutes until bubbly. Add milk, honey, olive oil, and salt and mix well. Stir in whole-wheat flour, cornmeal, and ½ cup bread flour; beat for 1 minute.
2. Stir in enough bread flour to make a firm dough. Turn onto floured surface and knead for 10 minutes. Place dough in greased bowl, turning to grease top. Cover and let rise for 1 hour.
3. Turn dough onto floured work surface and let rest for 10 minutes. Spray two 12″ round pizza pans with nonstick cooking spray and sprinkle with some cornmeal. Divide dough in half and roll to 12″ circles; place on pizza pans; press to edges if necessary. Let stand for 10 minutes.
4. Preheat oven to 400ºF. Bake crusts for 10 minutes or until set. Remove from oven, add toppings, return to oven, and bake as the pizza recipe directs.

Nutrition Info:

- Info Per Serving: Calories:213.01; Fat:3.17 g ;Saturated fat:0.46g ;Sodium: 104.52 mg

Apple-cinnamon Smoothie

Servings: 2
Cooking Time: X
Ingredients:

- 1 cup applesauce
- ½ cup vanilla yogurt
- ½ teaspoon cinnamon
- 1 apple, peeled and chopped
- 4 ice cubes

Directions:

1. Place applesauce, yogurt, cinnamon, and apple in blender or food processor; blend or process until smooth. Add ice cubes; blend or process until thick. Pour into glasses and serve immediately.

- Info Per Serving: Calories: 179.68; Fat: 1.08 g ;Saturated fat:0.55 g ;Sodium: 44.25 mg

French Toast With Citrus Compote

Servings: 4–6
Cooking Time: X

Ingredients:

- 1 orange
- 1 red grapefruit
- ½ cup sugar, divided
- 1 cup orange juice, divided
- 1 teaspoon vanilla
- 1 egg
- 6 slices Hearty-Grain French Bread
- 2 tablespoons butter or margarine

Directions:

1. Peel and chop orange and grapefruit and place in small bowl. In small saucepan, combine ¼ cup sugar with ½ cup orange juice and bring to a simmer. Simmer for 5–6 minutes or until slightly thickened; pour over orange mixture and set aside.

2. In shallow bowl, combine remaining ¼ cup sugar with ½ cup orange juice, vanilla, and egg, and beat well. Heat a nonstick pan over medium heat and add butter.

3. Slice bread on an angle. Dip bread into egg mixture, turning to coat. Cook in hot butter over medium heat for 6–8 minutes, turning once, until bread is crisp and deep golden brown. Serve with citrus compote.

Nutrition Info:

- Info Per Serving: Calories:262.24 ; Fat:4.59 g ;Saturated fat:2.07 g ;Sodium: 96.68 mg

Buckwheat Pancakes

Servings: 4
Cooking Time: X

Ingredients:

- ½ cup buttermilk
- 2 tablespoons butter or margarine, melted
- 2 egg whites
- ½ cup buckwheat flour
- ½ cup all-purpose flour
- 1½ teaspoons baking powder
- ½ teaspoon baking soda
- 3 tablespoons sugar Nonstick cooking spray

Directions:

1. In small bowl, combine buttermilk, butter, and egg white, and beat well. Set aside.

2. In large bowl, combine buckwheat flour, all-purpose flour, baking powder, baking soda, and sugar and mix well. Form a well in the center of the dry ingredients and add the wet ingredients. Stir just until batter is mixed; do not overmix.

3. Spray a skillet or griddle with nonstick cooking spray and heat over medium heat. Using a ¼-cup measure, pour four pancakes at once onto the griddle. Cook until bubbles form on the surface and begin to break. Flip pancakes and cook for 1–2 minutes on second side. Serve immediately.

Nutrition Info:

- Info Per Serving: Calories:215.98 ; Fat: 6.67 g ;Saturated fat: 3.94 g ;Sodium:350.46 mg

Spinach Artichoke Pizza

Servings: 8
Cooking Time: X

Ingredients:

- 1 (10-ounce) package frozen chopped spinach, thawed and drained
- 1 (9-ounce) package frozen artichoke hearts, thawed and drained
- 1 tablespoon olive oil
- 1 onion, chopped
- 3 cloves garlic, minced
- 1 red bell pepper, chopped
- 1 (8-ounce) package sliced mushrooms
- 1 cup part-skim ricotta cheese
- ¼ cup grated Parmesan cheese
- 1 cup shredded part-skim mozzarella cheese
- ½ cup shredded extra-sharp Cheddar cheese
- 1 Whole-Grain Pizza Crust

Directions:

1. Preheat oven to 400ºF. Press spinach between paper towels to remove all excess moisture. Cut artichoke hearts into small pieces.

2. In large saucepan, heat olive oil. Cook onion, garlic, red pepper, and mushrooms until crisp-tender, about 4 minutes. Add spinach; cook and stir until liquid evaporates, about 5 minutes longer. Add mushrooms; cook and stir for 2–3 minutes longer.

3. Drain vegetable mixture if necessary. Place in medium bowl and let cool for 20 minutes. Then blend in ricotta and Parmesan cheeses.

4. Spread on pizza crust. Top with mozzarella and Cheddar cheeses. Bake for 20–25 minutes or until pizza is hot and cheese is melted and begins to brown. Serve immediately.

Nutrition Info:

- Info Per Serving: Calories: 335.56; Fat:13.05 g ;Saturated fat: 6.06 g ;Sodium: 317.04 mg

Apple Pie Spice Soufflé

Servings: 4
Cooking Time: X
Ingredients:

- 1 cup applesauce
- ½ cup finely chopped apple
- 2 tablespoons brown sugar
- 2 tablespoons lemon juice
- ½ teaspoon cinnamon
- ¼ teaspoon nutmeg
- 1/8 teaspoon cloves
- ¼ teaspoon salt
- 1 egg yolk 8 egg whites
- ½ teaspoon cream of tartar
- 3 tablespoons sugar

Directions:

1. Preheat oven to 400ºF. In medium bowl, combine applesauce, apple, brown sugar, lemon juice, cinnamon, nutmeg, cloves, salt, and egg yolk and mix well.
2. In large bowl, combine egg whites with cream of tartar; beat until foamy. Gradually add sugar, beating until very stiff peaks form. Fold into apple mixture.
3. Spray the bottom of a 2-quart soufflé dish with nonstick cooking spray; pour apple mixture into dish. Bake for 45–50 minutes or until soufflé is puffed and deep golden brown. Serve immediately.

Nutrition Info:

- Info Per Serving: Calories: 181.22; Fat:1.29 g ;Saturated fat:0.41 g ;Sodium: 260.92 mg

Whole-grain Oatmeal Bread

Servings: 32
Cooking Time: X
Ingredients:

- 1 cup warm water
- 2 (¼-ounce) packages active dry yeast
- ¼ cup honey
- 1 cup skim milk
- 1 cup oatmeal
- 1 teaspoon salt
- 3 tablespoons canola oil
- 1 egg
- 1½ cups whole-wheat flour
- ½ cup medium rye flour
- ¼ cup ground flaxseed
- 3 to 4 cups bread flour
- 2 tablespoons butter

Directions:

1. In small bowl, combine water and yeast; let stand until bubbly, about 5 minutes. Meanwhile, in medium saucepan combine honey, milk, oatmeal, salt, and canola oil. Heat just until very warm (about 120ºF). Remove from heat and beat in egg. Combine in large bowl with whole-wheat flour, rye flour, flaxseed, and 1 cup bread flour. Add yeast mixture and beat for 1 minute. Cover and let rise for 30 minutes.
2. Gradually stir in enough remaining bread flour to make a firm dough. Turn onto floured surface and knead until dough is elastic, about 10 minutes. Place in greased bowl, turning to grease top. Cover and let rise for 1 hour. Punch down dough, divide in half, and form into loaves. Place in greased 9″ × 5″ loaf pans, cover, and let rise for 30 minutes.
3. Bake in preheated 350ºF oven for 25–30 minutes or until golden brown. Brush with butter, then remove to wire racks to cool.

Nutrition Info:

- Info Per Serving: Calories: 136.74; Fat:3.46 g ;Saturated fat: 0.77 g ;Sodium: 85.39 mg

Cashew & Berry Shake

Servings: 2
Cooking Time: 5 Min
Ingredients:

- 2 cups fresh or frozen berries (your choice)
- 1¾ cups unsweetened cashew milk
- 1 cup fresh or frozen spinach, roughly chopped
- ¼ cup cashew butter
- ½ cup ice cubes

Directions:

1. In a blender, add the berries of choice, cashew milk, spinach, and cashew butter. Blend until lump-free and smooth.
2. Add the ice cubes and blend until smooth.

Nutrition Info:

- Info Per Serving: Calories: 324 ; Fat: 22g ;Saturated fat: 1 g ;Sodium: 186 mg

Protein Cereal

Servings: 4
Cooking Time: 20 Min
Ingredients:

- 1¾ cups water
- 1 cup quinoa
- Pinch fine sea salt
- 1 cup raisins
- ½ cup almonds, roughly chopped
- 1 cup unsweetened almond milk
- 4 tsp organic honey

Directions:

1. In a medium stockpot, add the water, quinoa, and salt, allow to boil.
2. Bring the heat down to low and simmer, covered, for 15 minutes, or until the water is absorbed. Remove from the heat and let it rest for 5 minutes.
3. Add the raisins and almonds, mix to combine.

4. Place a ¾ cup of the quinoa mixture into 4 bowls and pour a ¼ cup of almond milk in each bowl. Drizzle each bowl of quinoa with 1 tsp of organic honey.

Nutrition Info:
- Info Per Serving: Calories: 313 ; Fat: 10 g ;Saturated fat: 1 g ;Sodium: 33 mg

Crisp Polenta Open-faced Sandwiches

Servings: 8-10
Cooking Time: X

Ingredients:
- 1 recipe Cheese Polenta
- 1 cup shredded Gruyère cheese
- ¼ cup chopped fresh basil leaves
- 3 tomatoes, sliced
- 7 tablespoons grated Parmesan cheese

Directions:
1. Prepare polenta as directed, except when done, pour onto a greased cookie sheet; spread to a ½″ thick rectangle, about 9″ × 15″. Cover and chill until very firm, about 2 hours.
2. Preheat broiler. Cut polenta into fifteen 3″ squares. Place on broiler pan; broil for 4–6 minutes or until golden brown. Carefully turn polenta and broil for 3–5 minutes or until golden brown.
3. Remove from oven and sprinkle with Gruyère and basil. Top each with a slice of tomato, then Parmesan. Return to broiler and broil for 3–6 minutes or until cheese melts and sandwiches are hot. Serve immediately.

Nutrition Info:
- Info Per Serving: Calories: 176.21; Fat:7.80 g ;Saturated fat:4.53 g ;Sodium: 228.89 mg

Egg White And Avocado Breakfast Wrap

Servings: 1
Cooking Time: 6 Minutes

Ingredients:
- 2 teaspoons olive oil
- ½ red pepper, seeded and sliced
- ½ cup liquid egg whites
- ¼ avocado, pitted and sliced
- 2 tablespoons Fresh Lime Salsa
- 1 (6½-inch) whole wheat tortilla (or pita)

Directions:
1. In a medium skillet, heat the olive oil over medium-high heat. Add the red pepper and cook for 3 minutes until slightly soft, then remove and set aside.
2. In the same skillet over medium-high heat, scramble the egg whites until cooked through and no longer runny, about 3 minutes, then remove from heat.

3. Spread the scrambled eggs, cooked red peppers, avocado, and Fresh Lime Salsa over the tortilla.
4. Wrap up the tortilla and serve immediately.

Nutrition Info:
- Info Per Serving: Calories:407 ; Fat: 21g ;Saturated fat: 5g ;Sodium: 488mg

Cowheat-bread Tuna Melt

Servings: 4–6
Cooking Time: X

Ingredients:
- 1 tablespoon olive oil
- ½ cup chopped onion
- 1 clove garlic, minced
- 1 green bell pepper, chopped
- 1 (6-ounce) can solid white tuna, drained
- ½ cup chopped celery
- ¼ cup plain yogurt
- 2 tablespoons low-fat mayonnaise
- 1 tablespoon Dijon mustard
- 1/8 teaspoon white pepper
- 1 tomato
- 4 slices Whole-Grain Oatmeal Bread (page 63)
- ½ cup shredded Swiss cheese
- ¼ cup grated Parmesan cheese

Directions:
1. In a small saucepan, heat olive oil over medium heat. Add onion, garlic, and bell pepper; cook and stir until crisp-tender, about 4 minutes. Remove from heat and pour into medium bowl.
2. Add tuna, celery, yogurt, mayonnaise, mustard, and pepper and mix well.
3. Toast bread on both sides. Spread with tuna mixture. Top each sandwich with a tomato slice and sprinkle with cheeses.
4. Preheat broiler. Broil sandwiches 6″ from heat for 5–7 minutes or until sandwiches are hot and cheese melts and begins to brown. Cut in half and serve

Nutrition Info:
- Info Per Serving: Calories:240.86 ; Fat: 10.66 g ;Saturated fat:3.70 g ;Sodium: 309.57 mg

Cohawaiian Pizza

Servings: 6–8
Cooking Time: X

Ingredients:
- 1 tablespoon olive oil
- 1 onion, chopped
- 3 cloves garlic, minced
- 1 green bell pepper, chopped
- 1 cup Spaghetti Sauce
- 1 Whole-Grain Pizza Crust , prebaked
- 1 (20-ounce) can pineapple tidbits, drained

- 1 cup chopped Canadian bacon
- 1 cup part-skim mozzarella cheese

Directions:

1. Preheat oven to 400ºF. In large saucepan, heat olive oil over medium heat. Add onion, garlic, and green pepper; cook and stir until crisp-tender, about 4 minutes. Remove from heat and mix in Spaghetti Sauce.

2. Place pizza crust on baking sheet and top with sauce mixture. Drain pineapple tidbits and pat dry between paper towels. Arrange pineapple and Canadian bacon on top of crust. Sprinkle with mozzarella.

3. Bake at 400ºF for 20–30 minutes or until pizza is hot and cheese is melted and beginning to brown. Serve immediately.

Nutrition Info:

- Info Per Serving: Calories: 300.45; Fat:6.94 g ;Saturated fat: 2.56 g;Sodium: 365.23 mg

Nutty Oat Bars

Servings: 6
Cooking Time: 7 Minutes

Ingredients:

- Olive oil
- 1 cup pitted Medjool dates
- 1 cup steel-cut oats
- ½ cup nut butter (such as almond, cashew, or all-natural peanut butter)
- 2 tablespoons maple syrup
- ½ cup almonds

Directions:

1. Lightly coat a 4-by-8-inch baking pan with olive oil.

2. In a blender or food processor, process the dates until a paste forms, about 2 minutes.

3. Place the oats in a medium skillet over low heat and toast for 5 minutes or until the edges turn brown. Set aside.

4. In a medium saucepan, combine the nut butter and maple syrup over medium heat, and cook for 1 to 2 minutes, stirring with a wooden spoon.

5. In a medium bowl, mix the date paste, oats, nut butter mixture, and almonds until everything is coated well.

6. Press the oat mixture into the prepared baking pan and place it in the freezer until it sets, about 20 minutes.

7. Once set, cut into six bars and serve.

Nutrition Info:

- Info Per Serving: Calories:379; Fat: 19g ;Saturated fat: 1g ;Sodium: 3mg

Baked French Toast Strips With Mixed Berry Sauce

Servings: 4
Cooking Time: 15 Minutes

Ingredients:

- 4 slices whole-wheat or gluten-free bread
- ½ cup low-fat soy or dairy milk
- 2 teaspoons brown sugar
- 1 egg
- 1 egg white
- 1 teaspoon vanilla extract
- ½ cup raspberries
- ½ cup sliced strawberries
- 1 tablespoon orange juice

Directions:

1. Preheat the oven to 375°F. Line a baking sheet with parchment paper.

2. Cut the bread into four strips each; set aside.

3. In a shallow bowl, combine the milk, brown sugar, egg, egg white, and vanilla, and beat until frothy.

4. Dip the bread strips into the milk mixture, turning once. Let the strips sit in the egg mixture for 1 minute. Remove and place on the prepared baking sheet.

5. Bake the strips for 15 to 20 minutes, until crisp and golden brown.

6. Meanwhile, combine the raspberries, strawberries, and orange juice in a small bowl. Mash until combined. (You can also prepare this sauce in a blender.)

7. When the French toast strips are done, serve immediately with the sauce on the side.

Nutrition Info:

- Info Per Serving: Calories: 131 ; Fat: 3 g ;Saturated fat: 1 g ;Sodium: 182 mg

Apple-cinnamon Quinoa

Servings: 1
Cooking Time: 12 Minutes

Ingredients:

- 1¼ cups low-fat milk
- 1 cup diced apple, divided
- ½ cup quinoa
- 1 teaspoon ground cinnamon
- 1 teaspoon maple syrup

Directions:

1. In a medium saucepan over medium heat, place the milk, ½ cup of apple, the quinoa, and cinnamon and bring to a boil. Reduce the heat to low, partially cover, and simmer until all the liquid evaporates, about 12 minutes.

2. Transfer the quinoa mixture to a bowl and top with the remaining diced apple and maple syrup. Serve.

Nutrition Info:

Hearty-grain French Bread

Servings: 32
Cooking Time: X
Ingredients:
- 1 cup quick-cooking oats
- 1 cup water
- ½ cup cottage cheese
- ½ cup low-fat sour cream
- 2 tablespoons orange juice
- ½ teaspoon salt
- 2 cups bread flour
- 2 (¼-ounce) packages instant-blend dry yeast
- ¼ cup oat bran
- 2 to 3 cups whole wheat flour
- 2 tablespoons cornmeal

Directions:
1. In small microwave-safe bowl, combine oats and 1 cup water; microwave on high for 3–4 minutes until creamy. Let cool for 10 minutes. Then combine oatmeal mixture and cottage cheese in a blender or food processor; blend or process until creamy.
2. Place oatmeal mixture in large bowl and stir in sour cream, orange juice, and salt; mix well. Add bread flour, yeast, and oat bran and beat for one minute. Then stir in enough whole wheat flour to form a firm dough.
3. Knead dough on lightly floured surface until smooth and elastic, about 8 minutes. Place dough in greased bowl, turning to grease top. Cover and let rise until doubled, about 1 hour.
4. Punch down dough and place on counter. Cover with bowl and let stand for 10 minutes. Grease two 12″ long rectangles on a cookie sheet and sprinkle with cornmeal. Divide dough into two balls. Roll each ball into a 12″ cylinder and place on prepared cookie sheet. Cover and let rise until doubled, about 30 minutes.
5. Preheat oven to 375ºF. Spray loaves with some cold water and bake for 30–40 minutes or until loaves are deep golden brown and sound hollow when tapped with fingers. Cool on wire rack.

Nutrition Info:
- Info Per Serving: Calories:94.80 ; Fat:1.23 g ;Saturated fat:0.43 g ;Sodium: 53.23 mg

Open-faced Tomato-basil Sandwiches

Servings: 8
Cooking Time: X
Ingredients:
- 3 tablespoons olive oil, divided
- 4 tomatoes, chopped
- ¼ cup chopped fresh basil
- 1 teaspoon fresh oregano leaves
- 2 cloves garlic, minced Pinch salt
- 1/8 teaspoon white pepper
- 12 slices Hearty-Grain French Bread
- 1 cup shredded Havarti cheese

Directions:
1. In small bowl, combine 1 tablespoon olive oil, tomatoes, basil, oregano, and garlic and mix well. Sprinkle with salt and pepper, stir, and set aside.
2. Preheat broiler. Brush bread slices on one side with remaining olive oil. Place, oil side up, on broiler pan. Broil 6″ from heat for 2–5 minutes or until bread is lightly toasted. Turn bread.
3. Sprinkle cheese on untoasted side of bread slices. Return to broiler and broil for 3–4 minutes or until cheese is melted and bubbling. Remove from broiler and immediately top each open-faced sandwich with a spoonful of the tomato mixture. Serve immediately.

Nutrition Info:
- Info Per Serving: Calories: 262.27; Fat:11.62 g ;Saturated fat: 4.03g;Sodium: 151.05 mg

Pork-and-slaw Sandwiches

Servings: 4
Cooking Time: X
Ingredients:
- 6 slices Herb-Crusted Pork Tenderloin
- 2 cups Apple Coleslaw
- 4 Ciabatta Rolls

Directions:
1. Using two forks, shred the tenderloin. Cut rolls in half. Place half of the coleslaw on the cut sides of the bread, and add the tenderloin. Top with remaining coleslaw, then remaining bun halves. Serve immediately.

Nutrition Info:
- Info Per Serving: Calories:474.96; Fat:16.35g ;Saturated fat:2.90 g ;Sodium:367.73 mg

Scrambled Egg Tacos

Servings: 4
Cooking Time: 10 Minutes
Ingredients:

- 1 whole egg
- 6 egg whites
- 1 tablespoon water
- 1 to 2 teaspoons chili powder
- Pinch salt
- ⅛ teaspoon black pepper
- ⅛ teaspoon red pepper flakes
- 1 teaspoon olive oil
- 4 warmed crisp corn taco shells, or 4 warmed corn or flour tortillas
- ⅔ cup salsa
- ¾ cup frozen corn, thawed
- 2 tablespoons grated cotija cheese
- 1 cup shredded romaine lettuce

Directions:

1. In a medium bowl, combine the egg, egg whites, water, chili powder, salt, pepper, and red pepper flakes, and beat thoroughly with a fork until foamy.
2. Heat the olive oil in a medium skillet over medium heat. Add the egg mixture and cook, stirring frequently, until the eggs are cooked through but still moist, about 5 to 7 minutes. Remove from the heat.
3. Meanwhile, warm the taco shells as directed on the package.
4. Divide the egg mixture among the taco shells and top with the salsa, corn, cheese, and lettuce. Serve immediately.

Nutrition Info:

- Info Per Serving: Calories: 166 ; Fat: 4 g ;Saturated fat: 1 g ;Sodium: 413 mg

Avocado And Kiwi Green Smoothies

Servings: X
Cooking Time: X
Ingredients:

- 1 cup unsweetened apple juice
- 1 avocado, cubed
- 1 cup roughly chopped kale
- 1 kiwi, peeled and chopped
- ½ cup coconut water or water
- 2 tablespoons honey
- 1 tablespoon chopped fresh basil
- 1 tablespoon chopped fresh mint

Directions:

1. In a blender, add the apple juice, avocado, kale, kiwi, coconut water, honey, basil, and mint and blend until very smooth.
2. Pour into glasses and serve immediately.

Nutrition Info:

- Info Per Serving: Calories: 308 ; Fat:14 g ;Saturated fat: 2 g ;Sodium: 28 mg

Cream-cheese Cinnamon Rolls

Servings: 32
Cooking Time: X
Ingredients:

- 1 recipe Honey-Wheat Sesame Bread
- 1 (8-ounce) package nonfat cream cheese, softened, divided
- 2 tablespoons butter or plant sterol margarine, softened
- ¼ cup brown sugar
- 1 cup dried blueberries
- 1 cup chopped hazelnuts
- 1 cup powdered sugar
- 2 tablespoons milk
- 1 teaspoon vanilla

Directions:

1. Prepare the bread dough, omitting sesame seeds. Let rise once, then punch down and let rest for 10 minutes.
2. In small bowl, combine 6 ounces cream cheese with butter and beat until combined. Spray a large cookie sheet with nonstick cooking spray and set aside.
3. Divide dough in half and roll out dough on lightly floured surface to two 16″ × 7″ rectangles. Spread with cream cheese mixture. Sprinkle with brown sugar, blueberries, and hazelnuts. Roll up tightly, starting with long side.
4. Cut each roll into 16″ pieces. Place, cut side up, on prepared cookie sheet. Let rise for 30 minutes.
5. Preheat oven to 350ºF. Bake rolls for 15–20 minutes or until golden brown. Remove to wire rack to cool.
6. While rolls are still warm, combine remaining 2 ounces cream cheese, powdered sugar, vanilla, and 1 tablespoon milk in small bowl and beat well. Add more milk if necessary to make frosting consistency. Frost warm rolls, then cool completely.

Nutrition Info:

- Info Per Serving: Calories:215.29; Fat:6.06g ;Saturated fat: 1.72 g ;Sodium:81.90 mg

Poultry

Cold Chicken With Cherry Tomato Sauce

Servings: 3
Cooking Time: X

Ingredients:

- 2 teaspoons fresh thyme leaves
- ½ cup Low-Sodium Chicken Broth
- 12 ounces boneless, skinless chicken breasts
- 1 tablespoon olive oil
- 3 cloves garlic, minced
- 2 cups cherry tomatoes
- ½ cup no-salt tomato juice
- ½ cup chopped fresh basil
- ¼ cup low-fat sour cream
- 1/8 teaspoon white pepper

Directions:

1. In large saucepan, combine thyme and chicken broth; bring to a simmer over medium heat. Add chicken and reduce heat to low. Cover and poach for 7–9 minutes or until chicken is thoroughly cooked.
2. Place chicken in a casserole dish just large enough to hold the chicken. Pour poaching liquid over, then cover and refrigerate for at least 8 hours.
3. When ready to eat, heat olive oil in large skillet. Add garlic; cook and stir for 1 minute. Then stir in cherry tomatoes; cook and stir until the tomatoes pop, about 4–6 minutes. Add tomato juice, basil, sour cream, and pepper; stir, and heat briefly.
4. Slice the chicken and fan out on serving plate. Top with tomato mixture and serve immediately.

Nutrition Info:

- Info Per Serving: Calories: 227.58; Fat: 8.63 g ;Saturated fat: 2.57 g ;Sodium: 198.32 mg

Chicken Breasts With Salsa

Servings: 4
Cooking Time: X

Ingredients:

- 2 tablespoons lime juice, divided
- 1 egg white
- 1 cup whole-grain cereal, crushed
- 1 teaspoon dried thyme leaves
- ¼ teaspoon pepper
- 4 (4-ounce) boneless, skinless chicken breasts
- 1 cup Super Spicy Salsa
- 1 jalapeño pepper, minced

Directions:

1. Preheat oven to 375ºF. Line a cookie sheet with a wire rack and set aside. In small bowl, combine 1 tablespoon lime juice and egg white; beat until frothy. On shallow plate, combine crushed cereal, thyme, and pepper.
2. Dip chicken into egg white mixture, then into cereal mixture to coat. Place on prepared cookie sheet. Bake for 20–25 minutes or until chicken is thoroughly cooked and coating is crisp.
3. Meanwhile, in small saucepan combine remaining 1 tablespoon lime juice, salsa, and jalapeño pepper. Heat through, stirring occasionally. Serve with chicken.

Nutrition Info:

- Info Per Serving: Calories: 264.05; Fat: 4.43 g ;Saturated fat:1.18 g ;Sodium: 146.85 mg

Moroccan Chicken

Servings: 4
Cooking Time: 15 Minutes

Ingredients:

- 3 (4-ounce) boneless, skinless chicken thighs, cubed
- 1 teaspoon smoked paprika
- ½ teaspoon ground cinnamon
- ½ teaspoon ground cumin
- ⅛ teaspoon ground ginger
- 1 cup low-sodium chicken broth
- 2 tablespoons fresh lemon juice
- 1 tablespoon cornstarch
- 1 teaspoon olive oil
- 1 onion, chopped
- 3 cloves garlic, minced
- 2 cups sugar snap peas
- 1 cup shredded carrots

Directions:

1. Put the cubed chicken in a medium bowl. Sprinkle with the paprika, cinnamon, cumin, and ginger, and work the spices into the meat. Set aside.
2. In a small bowl, combine the chicken broth, lemon juice, and cornstarch and mix well. Set aside.
3. Heat the olive oil in a large nonstick skillet over medium-high heat. Add the chicken thighs, and sauté for 5 minutes or until the chicken starts to brown. Remove the chicken from the pan and set aside.
4. Add the onion and garlic to the skillet, and sauté for 3 minutes.
5. Add the sugar snap peas and carrots to the skillet and sauté for 2 minutes.
6. Return the chicken to the skillet and stir. Add the chicken broth mixture, bring to a simmer, and turn down the heat to low. Simmer 3 to 4 minutes or until the sauce thickens, the vegetables are tender, and the chicken is cooked to 165ºF on a meat thermometer. Serve hot.

Nutrition Info:
- Info Per Serving: Calories: 165 ; Fat : 5 g ;Saturated fat: 1 g ;Sodium: 112 mg

Mini Turkey Meatloaves

Servings: 4
Cooking Time: 20 Minutes

Ingredients:
- ⅓ cup old-fashioned rolled oats
- 2 scallions, finely chopped
- 1 egg
- 3 tablespoons no-salt-added tomato paste, divided
- 2 teaspoons olive oil
- Pinch salt
- ⅛ teaspoon black pepper
- ½ teaspoon dried ground leaves
- 16 ounces 99% lean ground white turkey
- 2 tablespoons low-sodium mustard
- 1 tablespoon water

Directions:
1. Preheat the oven to 450°F. Line a baking sheet with aluminum foil.
2. In a large bowl, combine the oats, scallions, egg, 2 tablespoons of the tomato paste, olive oil, salt, pepper, and marjoram, and mix well.
3. Add the ground turkey, and mix gently with your hands until well combined.
4. Divide the mixture into fourths and shape into mini loaves. Place on the prepared baking sheet.
5. In a small bowl, combine the remaining 1 tablespoon tomato paste, the mustard, and water and mix well. Brush over the mini meatloaves.
6. Bake for 18 to 22 minutes or until the meatloaves register 165°F on a meat thermometer.

Nutrition Info:
- Info Per Serving: Calories: 205 ; Fat : 5 g ;Saturated fat: 1 g ;Sodium: 252 mg

Pineapple Curried Chicken

Servings: 4
Cooking Time: 15 Minutes

Ingredients:
- 3 (6-ounce) boneless, skinless chicken breasts, cubed
- 2 teaspoons curry powder
- 2 tablespoons cornstarch
- ⅛ teaspoon cayenne pepper
- 1 teaspoon olive oil
- 2 shallots, minced
- 3 cloves garlic, minced
- 1 (16-ounce) can pineapple chunks, drained, reserving juice
- 2 teaspoons yellow curry paste (optional)
- ⅓ cup reserved pineapple juice
- 1 tablespoon fresh lemon juice
- 3 tablespoons plain nonfat Greek yogurt

Directions:
1. In a medium bowl, toss the chicken breast cubes with the curry powder, cornstarch, and cayenne pepper, and set aside.
2. In a large nonstick skillet, heat the olive oil over medium heat.
3. Add the shallots and garlic, and cook for 2 minutes, stirring frequently.
4. Add the coated chicken cubes. Cook and stir for 5 to 6 minutes or until the chicken starts to brown.
5. Add the pineapple chunks, yellow curry paste (if using), reserved pineapple juice, and lemon juice to the skillet and bring to a simmer.
6. Simmer for 3 to 4 minutes or until the chicken is cooked to 165°F when tested with a meat thermometer. Stir in the yogurt and serve hot.

Nutrition Info:
- Info Per Serving: Calories: 260 ; Fat : 3 g ;Saturated fat: 1 g ;Sodium: 93 mg

Lemon Tarragon Turkey Medallions

Servings: 4
Cooking Time: 10 Minutes

Ingredients:
- 1 pound turkey tenderloin
- Pinch salt
- ⅛ teaspoon lemon pepper
- 2 tablespoons cornstarch
- 1 teaspoon dried tarragon leaves
- ¼ cup fresh lemon juice
- ½ cup low-sodium chicken stock
- 1 teaspoon grated fresh lemon zest
- 2 teaspoons olive oil

Directions:
1. Cut the turkey tenderloin crosswise into ½-inch slices. Sprinkle with the salt and lemon pepper.
2. In a small bowl, combine the cornstarch, tarragon, lemon juice, chicken stock, and lemon zest, and mix well.
3. Heat the olive oil in a large nonstick skillet over medium heat.
4. Add the turkey tenderloins. Cook for 2 minutes, and then turn and cook for another 2 minutes.
5. Add the lemon juice mixture to the skillet. Cook, stirring frequently, until the sauce boils and thickens and the turkey is cooked to 165°F on a meat thermometer. Serve immediately.

Nutrition Info:
- Info Per Serving: Calories: 169 ; Fat :3 g ;Saturated fat: 1 g ;Sodium: 77 mg

Turkey With Prunes

Servings: 6
Cooking Time: X
Ingredients:

- 3 tablespoons olive oil
- 1 onion, chopped
- 3 cloves garlic, minced
- 1 cup finely chopped pitted prunes
- 1/8 teaspoon salt
- 1/8 teaspoon pepper
- ½ cup chopped hazelnuts
- 6 (3-ounce) turkey cutlets
- 2 tablespoons flour
- ½ cup Low-Sodium Chicken Broth
- ¼ cup dry white wine
- ½ teaspoon dried thyme leaves
- 1 tablespoon lemon juice

Directions:

1. In small saucepan, heat 1 tablespoon olive oil over medium heat. Add onion and garlic; cook and stir until crisp-tender, about 4 minutes. Add prunes and sprinkle with salt and pepper. Cook for 3–4 minutes or until prunes begin to plump. Add nuts and remove from heat. Let cool for 20 minutes.
2. Arrange turkey cutlets on work surface. Divide prune mixture among the cutlets. Roll up, securing with kitchen twine or toothpicks. Dredge filled cutlets in flour.
3. Heat remaining 2 tablespoons olive oil in large skillet. Brown turkey, turning to cook evenly, for about 4–5 minutes. Then add broth, wine, and thyme leaves to skillet. Cover and braise cutlets for 6–8 minutes or until turkey is tender and thoroughly cooked. Add lemon juice and serve immediately.

Nutrition Info:

- Info Per Serving: Calories: 327.80; Fat: 15.34 g ;Saturated fat: 2.04 g;Sodium: 92.23 mg

Turkey Breast With Dried Fruit

Servings: 6
Cooking Time: X
Ingredients:

- 1½ pounds bone-in turkey breast
- 1/8 teaspoon salt
- 1/8 teaspoon pepper
- 1 tablespoon flour
- 1 tablespoon olive oil
- 1 tablespoon butter or plant sterol margarine
- ½ cup chopped prunes
- ½ cup chopped dried apricots
- 2 Granny Smith apples, peeled and chopped
- 1 cup Low-Sodium Chicken Broth
- ¼ cup Madeira wine

Directions:

1. Sprinkle turkey with salt, pepper, and flour. In large saucepan, heat olive oil and butter over medium heat. Add turkey and cook until browned, about 5 minutes. Turn turkey.
2. Add all fruit to saucepan along with broth and wine. Cover and bring to a simmer. Reduce heat to medium low and simmer for 55–65 minutes or until turkey is thoroughly cooked. Serve turkey with fruit and sauce.

Nutrition Info:

- Info Per Serving: Calories: 293.15; Fat: 6.01 g ;Saturated fat: 1.94 g ;Sodium: 127.28 mg

Piña Colada Chicken

Servings: 2
Cooking Time: 20 Min
Ingredients:

- Aluminum foil
- 2 (4 oz) chicken breasts, pounded flat
- 2 tsp unsweetened coconut flakes
- 1 (20 oz) can crushed pineapple, drained
- 1 cup green bell peppers, diced
- ¼ cup soy sauce

Directions:

1. Heat the oven to 400°F gas mark 6. Line a baking sheet with aluminum foil.
2. Place the chicken breasts on the baking sheet and top with coconut flakes.
3. Place the pineapple and green bell peppers around the chicken breasts.
4. Drizzle the chicken breasts with soy sauce and cook for 10 to 15 minutes, until the pineapple is caramelised, and the chicken is cooked through. Serve warm.

Nutrition Info:

- Info Per Serving: Calories: 327 ; Fat: 6 g ;Saturated fat: 1 g ;Sodium: 206 mg

Grilled Turkey And Veggie Kabobs

Servings: 4
Cooking Time: 10 Minutes
Ingredients:

- 1 pound turkey tenderloin
- Pinch salt
- ⅛ teaspoon cayenne pepper
- 1 yellow summer squash, cut into ½-inch slices
- 1 orange bell pepper, seeded and cut into 1-inch cubes
- 1 red bell pepper, seeded and cut into 1-inch cubes
- 3 scallions, cut into 2-inch pieces
- ¼ cup apple jelly
- 2 tablespoons fresh lemon juice
- 1 tablespoon butter
- 1 tablespoon low-sodium mustard
- 1 teaspoon dried oregano leaves

Directions:

1. Prepare and preheat the grill to medium heat.

2. Cut the turkey into 1-inch cubes, put on a plate, and sprinkle with the salt and cayenne pepper.

3. Thread the turkey cubes, alternating with the squash, orange bell pepper, red bell pepper, and scallion, onto kabob skewers.

4. In a small saucepan, combine the apple jelly, lemon juice, and butter. Heat over low heat until the apple jelly melts and the mixture is smooth, about 2 minutes. Stir in the mustard and oregano.

5. Place the kabobs on the hot grill and brush with some of the apple jelly mixture. Cover and grill for 4 minutes.

6. Uncover, turn the kabobs, and brush with more of the apple jelly mixture. Cover and grill for 3 minutes.

7. Uncover the grill and turn the kabobs, brushing with the remaining apple jelly mixture, and cook until the turkey registers 165°F on a meat thermometer, 2 to 3 minutes longer. Use all of the apple jelly mixture; if any is left, discard it.

Nutrition Info:

- Info Per Serving: Calories: 232 ; Fat : 5 g ;Saturated fat: 2 g ;Sodium: 194 mg

Balsamic Blueberry Chicken

Servings: 2
Cooking Time: 25 Min
Ingredients:

- Aluminum foil
- ½ cup fresh blueberries
- 2 tbsp. pine nuts
- ¼ cup cilantro, chopped
- 2 tbsp. balsamic vinegar
- ¼ tsp ground black pepper
- 2 (4 oz) chicken breasts, butterflied

Directions:

1. Heat the olive oil in a medium-sized frying pan over medium Heat the oven to 375°F gas mark 5. Line a baking sheet with aluminum foil.

2. In a medium-sized mixing bowl, add the blueberries, pine nuts, cilantro, balsamic vinegar, and pepper, mix until well combined.

3. Place the chicken breasts on the baking sheet and pour the blueberry mixture on top.

4. Bake for 20 to 25 minutes, until the juices are caramelized, and the inside of the chicken has cooked through. Serve warm.

Nutrition Info:

- Info Per Serving: Calories: 212 ; Fat: 7 g ;Saturated fat:1 g ;Sodium: 58 mg

Mediterranean Patties

Servings: 4
Cooking Time: 15 Min
Ingredients:

- Aluminium foil
- 1 cup broccoli florets
- 1 small red onion, quartered
- ¼ cup black olives, pitted
- 8 oz baby spinach, roughly chopped
- 1 lb. ground chicken
- 1½ tsp Mediterranean Seasoning Rub Blend
- 4 whole wheat buns
- Lettuce
- Tomato

Directions:

1. Preheat the oven to broil. Line a baking sheet with aluminum foil.

2. In a food processor, pulse the broccoli, onion, and olives for 1 to 2 minutes, until minced.

3. In a large-sized mixing bowl, add the baby spinach, broccoli mixture, chicken, and the Mediterranean spice blend, mix to combine. Form into 8 medium-sized patties and place them on the baking sheet.

4. Broil for 10 minutes on one side, flip, then broil for 3 minutes on the other side until golden brown.

5. Serve on wholewheat buns with lettuce and tomato, or with a garden salad.

Nutrition Info:

- Info Per Serving: Calories: 206 ; Fat: 10 g ;Saturated fat: 3 g ;Sodium: 134 mg

Mixed Berry Chicken Salad

Servings: 4
Cooking Time: 8 Minutes
Ingredients:

- 4 (6-ounce) boneless, skinless chicken breasts, cubed
- Pinch salt
- ⅛ teaspoon white pepper
- 2 teaspoons olive oil, divided
- 2 cups sliced strawberries
- 2 cups blueberries
- 1 cup blackberries
- ⅓ cup low-fat plain Greek yogurt
- 3 tablespoons fresh lime juice
- 2 tablespoons honey
- 1 teaspoon grated fresh lime zest
- 1 cup raspberries
- 4 cups mixed green lettuce

Directions:

1. Sprinkle the chicken breasts with the salt and pepper.

2. Heat 1 teaspoon of the olive oil in a large nonstick skillet. Add the chicken and cook, stirring frequently, until

lightly browned and cooked to 165°F when tested with a meat thermometer, about 5 to 7 minutes. Transfer to a clean plate.

3. In a large bowl, combine the strawberries, blueberries, and blackberries, and gently toss to mix.

4. In a small bowl, combine the yogurt, lime juice, honey, lime zest, and remaining 1 teaspoon olive oil, and mix well.

5. Add the chicken to the berry mixture, and drizzle the yogurt mixture over all the ingredients. Toss gently.

6. Top the chicken salad with the raspberries. Serve on a bed of the mixed green lettuce.

Nutrition Info:

*   Info Per Serving: Calories: 394 ; Fat : 6 g ;Saturated fat: 1 g ;Sodium: 138 mg

Turkey Oat Patties

Servings: 6
Cooking Time: 30 Min
Ingredients:

*   Aluminum foil
*   1 lb. lean ground turkey
*   ½ cup rolled oats
*   ¼ cup sun-dried tomatoes julienne cut, drained
*   ¼ cup brown onion, finely chopped
*   ¼ cup parsley, finely chopped
*   1 tbsp. garlic, crushed
*   6 whole-wheat hamburger buns
*   1 ripe avocado, peeled, pitted, and mashed
*   6 iceberg lettuce leaves
*   6 Roma tomato slices
*   Hamburger dill pickle chips

Directions:

1. Preheat the oven to broil. Line a baking sheet with aluminum foil.

2. In a large-sized mixing bowl, add the turkey, oats, sun-dried tomatoes, onion, parsley, and garlic, mix to combine. Shape into 6 patties.

3. Place the turkey patties on the baking sheet, and broil for 3 to 4 minutes on each side, until fully cooked and the juices run clear.

4. Meanwhile, prepare a self-serving platter with the buns, mashed avocado, lettuce leaves, tomato slices, and the dill pickle chips. Assemble the way you like.

Nutrition Info:

*   Info Per Serving: Calories: 366 ; Fat: 15g;Saturated fat: 3 g ;Sodium: 52 mg

Turkey Cutlets Florentine

Servings: 6
Cooking Time: X
Ingredients:

*   1 egg white, beaten
*   ½ cup dry breadcrumbs
*   1/8 teaspoon white pepper
*   2 tablespoons grated Parmesan cheese
*   6 (4-ounce) turkey cutlets
*   2 tablespoons olive oil
*   2 cloves minced garlic
*   2 (8-ounce) bags fresh baby spinach
*   1/8 teaspoon ground nutmeg
*   1/3 cup shredded Jarlsberg cheese

Directions:

1. In shallow bowl, place egg white and beat until foamy. On shallow plate, combine breadcrumbs, pepper, and Parmesan and mix well.

2. Place turkey cutlets between waxed paper and pound to " thickness if necessary. Dip cutlets into egg white, then into breadcrumb mixture to coat.

3. In large saucepan, heat olive oil over medium-high heat. Add turkey; cook for 4 minutes. Carefully turn and cook for 4–6 minutes longer, until thoroughly cooked. Remove to serving plate and cover with foil to keep warm.

4. Add garlic to drippings remaining in pan; cook and stir for 1 minute. Then add spinach and nutmeg; cook and stir until spinach wilts, about 4–5 minutes. Add the Jarlsberg, top with the turkey, cover, and remove from heat. Let stand for 2 minutes to melt cheese, then serve.

Nutrition Info:

*   Info Per Serving: Calories: 258.57; Fat:9.19 g ;Saturated fat:2.15 g ;Sodium: 236.98mg

Turkey Tacos Verde

Servings: 4
Cooking Time: 13 Minutes
Ingredients:

*   1 teaspoon olive oil
*   1 pound 99% lean ground white turkey
*   1 onion, chopped
*   3 cloves garlic, minced
*   10 tomatillos, husk removed, rinsed and chopped
*   2 jalapeño peppers, seeded and minced
*   ½ cup low-sodium salsa verde
*   8 corn tortillas, warmed
*   ½ cup low-fat plain Greek yogurt
*   2 tablespoons chopped fresh cilantro
*   2 scallions, minced
*   2 cups mixed salad greens

Directions:

1. In a large nonstick skillet, heat the olive oil over medium heat.
2. Add the ground turkey, onion, and garlic and stir to break up the meat.
3. Sauté the mixture until the turkey is cooked through, about 5 to 6 minutes.
4. Add the tomatillos and jalapeño peppers and stir for 3 to 4 minutes. Then add the salsa verde and stir.
5. Meanwhile, combine the yogurt, cilantro, and scallions in a small bowl
6. Assemble the tacos starting with the tortillas, turkey mixture, yogurt mixture, and top with the salad greens. Serve immediately.

Nutrition Info:
- Info Per Serving: Calories:338 ; Fat : 6 g ;Saturated fat: 1 g ;Sodium: 295 mg

Iron Packed Turkey

Servings: 2
Cooking Time: 30 Min
Ingredients:
- 2 (3 oz) turkey breasts, boneless and skinless
- Himalayan pink salt
- Ground black pepper
- 3 tsp avocado oil, divided
- 1 ½ cups spinach, roughly chopped
- 1 ½ cups kale, roughly chopped
- 1 ½ cups Swiss chard, roughly chopped
- 1 ½ cups collard greens, roughly chopped
- 1 tsp garlic crushed

Directions:
1. Preheat the oven to 400°F gas mark 6.
2. Season the turkey breasts with salt and pepper to taste.
3. Heat 1 tsp of avocado oil in a large cast-iron frying pan over medium-high heat.
4. Add the turkey breasts and cook for 5 minutes on each side until browned. Remove the turkey breasts and set them aside.
5. Add the remaining 2 tsp of avocado oil to the pan and fry the spinach, kale, Swiss chard, collard greens and garlic for 3 minutes until they are slightly wilted.
6. Season the mixed greens with salt and pepper to taste, place the turkey breasts on the greens.
7. Place the cast iron frying pan in the oven and bake for 15 minutes until the turkey breasts are cooked through.
8. Serve warm

Nutrition Info:
- Info Per Serving: Calories: 113 ; Fat: 2 g ;Saturated fat: 0 g ;Sodium: 128 mg

Hawaiian Chicken Stir-fry

Servings: 4
Cooking Time: 10 Minutes
Ingredients:
- 1 (8-ounce) can crushed pineapple, undrained
- ⅓ cup water
- 2 tablespoons cornstarch
- 1 teaspoon brown sugar
- 1 teaspoon low-sodium tamari sauce
- ¼ teaspoon ground ginger
- ⅛ teaspoon cayenne pepper
- 2 tablespoons unsweetened shredded coconut
- 2 tablespoons chopped macadamia nuts
- 2 teaspoons olive oil
- 1 onion, chopped
- 1 red bell pepper, seeded and chopped
- 3 (6-ounce) boneless, skinless chicken breasts, cubed

Directions:
1. In a medium bowl, combine the pineapple, water, cornstarch, brown sugar, tamari, ginger, and cayenne pepper, and mix well. Set aside.
2. Place a large nonstick skillet or wok over medium heat. Add the coconut and macadamia nuts, and toast for 1 to 2 minutes, stirring constantly, until fragrant. Remove from the skillet and set aside.
3. Add the olive oil to the skillet and heat over medium-high heat. Add the onion and red bell pepper, and stir-fry for 2 to 3 minutes or until almost tender.
4. Add the chicken to the wok, and stir-fry for 3 to 4 minutes or until lightly browned.
5. Stir the sauce, add to the skillet, and stir fry for 1 to 2 minutes longer until the sauce thickens and the chicken registers at 165°F when tested with a meat thermometer.
6. Serve immediately, topped with the toasted coconut and macadamia nuts.

Nutrition Info:
- Info Per Serving: Calories: 301 ; Fat : 12 g ;Saturated fat: 4 g ;Sodium: 131 mg

Nutty Coconut Chicken With Fruit Sauce

Servings: 4
Cooking Time: 15 Minutes
Ingredients:
- ¼ cup ground almonds
- ⅓ cup unsweetened flaked coconut
- ¼ cup coconut flour
- Pinch salt
- ⅛ teaspoon white pepper
- 1 egg white
- 1 (16-ounce) package chicken tenders
- 1 cup sliced strawberries

- 1 cup raspberries
- ⅓ cup unsweetened white grape juice
- 1 tablespoon lemon juice
- ½ teaspoon dried thyme leaves
- ⅓ cup dried cherries

Directions:

1. Preheat the oven to 400°F. Place a wire rack on a baking sheet.

2. In a shallow plate, combine the ground almonds, flaked coconut, coconut flour, salt, and white pepper, and mix well.

3. In a shallow bowl, beat the egg white just until foamy.

4. Dip the chicken tenders into the egg white, then into the almond mixture to coat. Place on the wire rack as you work.

5. Bake the chicken tenders for 14 to 16 minutes or until the chicken is cooked to 165°F when tested with a meat thermometer.

6. While the chicken is baking, in a food processor or blender, combine the strawberries, raspberries, grape juice, lemon juice, and thyme leaves and process or blend until smooth.

7. Pour the mixture into a small saucepan, and add the dried cherries. Bring to a simmer over medium heat. Simmer for 3 minutes, then remove the pan from the heat and set aside.

8. Serve the chicken with the warm fruit sauce.

Nutrition Info:

- Info Per Serving: Calories: 281 ; Fat : 8 g ;Saturated fat: 3 g ;Sodium: 124 mg

Chicken Stir-fry With Napa Cabbage

Servings: 4
Cooking Time: X
Ingredients:

- 2 (5-ounce) boneless, skinless chicken breasts
- 2 tablespoons cornstarch
- 2 tablespoons lemon juice
- 1 tablespoon low-sodium soy sauce
- 1 cup Low-Sodium Chicken Broth
- 2 tablespoons peanut oil
- 4 cups shredded Napa cabbage
- 4 green onions, sliced
- 1 green bell pepper, sliced
- 1½ cups frozen edamame, thawed

Directions:

1. Cut chicken into 1″ pieces. In small bowl, combine cornstarch, lemon juice, soy sauce, and chicken broth. Add chicken and let stand for 15 minutes.

2. Heat oil in large skillet or wok. Drain chicken, reserving marinade. Add chicken to skillet; stir-fry until almost cooked, about 4 minutes. Remove chicken to a plate.

3. Add cabbage and green onions to skillet; stir fry until cabbage wilts, about 4 minutes. Add bell pepper and edamame; stir-fry for 3–5 minutes longer until hot.

4. Stir marinade and add to skillet along with chicken. Stir-fry until sauce bubbles and thickens and chicken is thoroughly cooked. Serve over hot cooked brown rice.

Nutrition Info:

- Info Per Serving: Calories:307.21; Fat: 14.90 g ;Saturated fat: 2.47 g ;Sodium:214.61 mg

Turkey Curry With Fruit

Servings: 6
Cooking Time: X
Ingredients:

- 6 (4-ounce) turkey cutlets
- 1 tablespoon flour
- 1 tablespoon plus
- 1 teaspoon curry powder, divided
- 1 tablespoon olive oil
- 2 pears, chopped
- 1 apple, chopped ½ cup raisins
- 1 tablespoon sugar
- 1/8 teaspoon salt
- 1/3 cup apricot jam

Directions:

1. Preheat oven to 350ºF. Spray a cookie sheet with sides with nonstick cooking spray. Arrange cutlets on prepared cookie sheet. In small bowl, combine flour, 1 tablespoon curry powder, and olive oil and mix well. Spread evenly over cutlets.

2. In medium bowl, combine pears, apple, raisins, sugar, salt, 1 teaspoon curry powder, and apricot jam, and mix well. Divide this mixture over the turkey cutlets.

3. Bake for 35–45 minutes or until turkey is thoroughly cooked and fruit is hot and caramelized. Serve immediately.

Nutrition Info:

- Info Per Serving: Calories: 371.52; Fat: 11.15 g ;Saturated fat: 2.80 g ;Sodium: 121.35 mg

Sautéed Chicken With Roasted Garlic Sauce

Servings: 4
Cooking Time: X
Ingredients:

- 1 head Roasted Garlic
- 1/3 cup Low-Sodium Chicken Broth
- ½ teaspoon dried oregano leaves
- 4 (4-ounce) boneless, skinless chicken breasts
- ¼ cup flour
- 1/8 teaspoon salt
- 1/8 teaspoon pepper
- ¼ teaspoon paprika
- 2 tablespoons olive oil

Directions:

1. Squeeze garlic cloves from the skins and combine in small saucepan with chicken broth and oregano leaves.

2. On shallow plate, combine flour, salt, pepper, and paprika. Dip chicken into this mixture to coat.

3. In large skillet, heat 2 tablespoons olive oil. At the same time, place the saucepan with the garlic mixture over medium heat. Add the chicken to the hot olive oil; cook for 5 minutes without moving. Then carefully turn chicken and cook for 4–7 minutes longer until chicken is thoroughly cooked.

4. Stir garlic sauce with wire whisk until blended. Serve with the chicken.

Nutrition Info:

- Info Per Serving: Calories: 267.01; Fat: 7.78g ;Saturated fat:1.65 g ;Sodium: 158.61 mg

Chicken Spicy Thai Style

Servings: 4
Cooking Time: X
Ingredients:

- 2 tablespoons lime juice
- 1 tablespoon low-sodium soy sauce
- ½ cup Low-Sodium Chicken Broth
- ¼ cup dry white wine
- ¼ cup natural peanut butter
- 2 tablespoons peanut oil
- 1 onion, chopped
- 4 cloves garlic, minced
- 3 (4-ounce) boneless, skinless chicken breasts, sliced
- 4 cups shredded Napa cabbage
- 1 cup shredded carrots

Directions:

1. In small bowl, combine lime juice, soy sauce, chicken broth, wine, and peanut butter and mix with wire whisk until blended. Set aside.

2. In wok or large skillet, heat peanut oil over medium-high heat. Add onion and garlic; stir-fry until crisp-tender, about 4 minutes. Add chicken; stir-fry until almost cooked, about 3 minutes. Add cabbage and carrots; stir-fry until cabbage begins to wilt, about 3–4 minutes longer.

3. Remove food from wok and return wok to heat. Add peanut butter mixture and bring to a simmer. Return chicken and vegetables to wok; stir fry until sauce bubbles and thickens and chicken is thoroughly cooked, about 3–4 minutes. Serve immediately.

Nutrition Info:

- Info Per Serving: Calories: 300.35; Fat:16.70 g ;Saturated fat:3.20 g;Sodium:309.32 mg

Chicken Poached In Tomato Sauce

Servings: 4
Cooking Time: X
Ingredients:

- 1 cup brown rice
- 2 cups water
- 2 tablespoons olive oil
- 1 onion, chopped
- 3 cloves garlic, minced
- 2 cups chopped plum tomatoes
- ½ teaspoon dried tarragon
- ¼ cup dry red wine
- 3 tablespoons no-salt tomato paste
- 1 cup Low-Sodium Chicken Broth
- 1/8 teaspoon salt
- 1/8 teaspoon pepper
- 3 (5-ounce) boneless, skinless chicken thighs, sliced

Directions:

1. In medium saucepan, combine rice and water and bring to a boil over high heat. Reduce heat to low, cover, and simmer for 30–40 minutes or until rice is tender.

2. Meanwhile, in large saucepan heat olive oil over medium heat. Add onion and garlic; cook and stir for 4 minutes until crisp-tender. Add tomatoes, tarragon, wine, tomato paste, chicken broth, salt, and pepper, and bring to a simmer, stirring frequently.

3. Add chicken and bring back to a simmer. Cover pan, reduce heat to low, and poach chicken for 15–20 minutes or until thoroughly cooked. Serve over hot cooked rice.

Nutrition Info:

- Info Per Serving: Calories: 285.33; Fat: 9.22g ;Saturated fat: 1.70 g;Sodium: 129.66 mg

Italian Chicken Bake

Servings: 4
Cooking Time: 25 Min
Ingredients:

- 1 lb. chicken breasts, halved lengthwise into 4 pieces
- ½ tsp garlic powder
- ½ tsp fine sea salt
- ¼ tsp ground black pepper
- ¼ tsp Italian seasoning
- ½ cup basil, finely chopped
- 4 part-skim mozzarella cheese slices
- 2 large Roma tomatoes, finely chopped

Directions:

1. Heat the oven to 400°F gas mark 6.

2. Season the cut chicken breasts with garlic powder, salt, pepper and Italian seasoning.

3. Place the seasoned chicken breasts on a baking sheet. Bake for 18 to 22 minutes, or until the chicken breasts are

cooked through. Remove from the oven and set it to broil on high.

4. Evenly place the basil, 1 mozzarella slice and tomatoes on each chicken breast.

5. Return the baking sheet to the oven and broil for 2 to 3 minutes, until the cheese has melted and browned.

6. Remove from the oven and serve hot.

Nutrition Info:

* Info Per Serving: Calories: 239 ; Fat: 9 g ;Saturated fat: 4 g ;Sodium: 524 mg

Lime Turkey Skewers

Servings: 4
Cooking Time: 15 Min
Ingredients:

* 1 lb. boneless, skinless turkey breasts, cut into chunks
* 1 lime, juiced
* 2 tbsp. avocado oil, plus 1 tbsp.
* 2 tbsp. garlic, minced
* 1 tsp dried thyme
* 1 tsp dried dill
* ½ tsp fine sea salt
* ¼ tsp ground black pepper

Directions:

1. In a medium-sized mixing bowl, add the turkey breasts, lime juice, avocado oil, garlic, thyme, dill, salt and pepper, mix to combine. Rest for 30 minutes in the fridge.

2. Thread the marinated turkey chunks onto 8 skewers.

3. Heat 1 tbsp. of avocado oil in a heavy-bottom pan over medium-high heat.

4. Place the skewers gently in the pan and fry for 5 to 7 minutes, flip, and cook for 5 to 8 minutes, or until the turkey is cooked through and no longer pink inside. Remove from the heat and serve.

Nutrition Info:

* Info Per Serving: Calories: 205 ; Fat: 10 g ;Saturated fat: 2 g ;Sodium: 343 mg

Mustard-roasted Almond Chicken Tenders

Servings: 4
Cooking Time: 15 Minutes
Ingredients:

* ¼ cup low-sodium yellow mustard
* 2 teaspoons yellow mustard seed
* ¼ teaspoon dry mustard
* ⅛ teaspoon garlic powder
* 1 egg white
* 2 tablespoons fresh lemon juice
* ¼ cup almond flour
* ¼ cup ground almonds
* 1 pound chicken tenders

Directions:

1. Preheat the oven to 400°F. Place a wire rack on a baking sheet.

2. In a shallow bowl, combine the yellow mustard, mustard seed, ground mustard, garlic powder, egg white, and lemon juice, and whisk well.

3. To a plate or shallow bowl, add the almond flour and ground almonds, and combine.

4. Dip the chicken tenders into the mustard-egg mixture, then into the almond mixture to coat. Place each tender on the rack on the baking pan as you work.

5. Bake the chicken for 12 to 15 minutes or until a meat thermometer registers 165°F. Serve immediately.

Nutrition Info:

* Info Per Serving: Calories: 166 ; Fat : 4 g ;Saturated fat: 0 g ;Sodium: 264 mg

One Pan Chicken

Servings: 4
Cooking Time: 30 Min
Ingredients:

* 2 tbsp. olive oil
* 4 bone-in chicken thighs, skin removed
* ¾ tsp Himalayan pink salt, divided
* ½ tsp ground black pepper, divided
* 1 (15 oz) can petite diced tomatoes, drained
* ¼ cup water
* 1 (14 oz) can asparagus cut spears, drained
* ¼ cup black olives, pitted
* ¼ cup cilantro, chopped

Directions:

1. Heat the oven to 350°F gas mark 4.

2. Heat the olive oil in a large oven-proof frying pan over a medium-high heat.

3. Season the chicken thighs with ¼ tsp of salt and ¼ tsp of pepper. Place the thighs in the frying pan and cook for 2 to 3 minutes per side, or until lightly browned, transfer to a plate.

4. In the same pan add the drained tomatoes and water and deglaze by scraping the bottom bits from the pan.

5. Add the asparagus, black olives, ½ tsp salt and ¼ tsp pepper, mix to combine.

6. Place the chicken thighs back into the pan and push them down into the tomato mixture.

7. Place the ovenproof pan in the oven and bake for 20 minutes, or until the chicken is fully cooked.

8. Remove from the oven and sprinkle with cilantro, serve warm.

Nutrition Info:

* Info Per Serving: Calories: 270 ; Fat: 13 g ;Saturated fat: 2 g ;Sodium: 514 mg

Hazelnut-crusted Chicken Breasts

Servings: 2
Cooking Time: X
Ingredients:
- 2 (4-ounce) boneless, skinless chicken breasts Pinch salt Pinch pepper
- 1 tablespoon Dijon mustard
- 1 egg white
- 1/3 cup chopped hazelnuts
- 1 tablespoon olive oil

Directions:
1. Place chicken between two sheets of waxed paper. Pound, starting at center of chicken, until ¼" thick. Sprinkle chicken with salt and pepper. Spread each side of chicken with some of the mustard.
2. In small bowl, beat egg white until foamy. Dip chicken into egg white, then into hazelnuts, pressing to coat both sides.
3. In skillet, heat olive oil over medium heat. Add chicken; cook for 3 minutes without moving. Then carefully turn and cook for 1–3 minutes on second side until chicken is thoroughly cooked and nuts are toasted. Serve immediately.

Nutrition Info:
- Info Per Serving: Calories: 276.64; Fat:16.02 g ;Saturated fat:1.88 g;Sodium: 266.25 mg

Piri Piri Chicken

Servings: 4
Cooking Time: 15 Minutes
Ingredients:
- 3 (6-ounce) boneless, skinless chicken breasts, cubed
- 2 tablespoons lemon juice
- 1 teaspoon smoked paprika
- ½ teaspoon cayenne pepper
- Pinch salt
- 2 teaspoons chili powder
- 1 teaspoon olive oil
- 1 onion, chopped
- 4 cloves garlic, minced
- 1 red bell pepper, chopped
- 1 red chile pepper, such as chile de arbol, seeded and minced
- 2 tablespoons Piri Piri sauce
- 1 cup low-sodium chicken broth
- 1 tablespoon cornstarch

Directions:
1. Place the chicken breasts in a medium bowl and drizzle with the lemon juice.
2. Sprinkle the chicken with the smoked paprika, cayenne pepper, salt, and chili powder. Work the spices into the chicken with your hands and set aside.
3. In a large nonstick skillet, heat the olive oil over medium heat.
4. Add the chicken to the skillet. Cook, stirring frequently, until the chicken is lightly browned, about 4 minutes. Transfer the chicken to a clean plate.
5. Add the onion, garlic, red bell pepper, red chile pepper, and Piri Piri sauce to the skillet stir. Sauté 3 to 4 minutes or until the vegetables are crisp-tender. Return the chicken to the skillet.
6. In a small bowl, combine the chicken broth and cornstarch and mix with a whisk. Stir into the chicken mixture.
7. Simmer 3 to 4 minutes or until the chicken is cooked to 165°F when tested with a meat thermometer, and the sauce is thickened. Serve immediately.

Nutrition Info:
- Info Per Serving: Calories: 209 ; Fat : 5 g ;Saturated fat: 1 g ;Sodium: 210 mg

Pork And Beef Mains

Pork Quesadillas

Servings: 6
Cooking Time: X
Ingredients:
- 1/3 cup low-fat sour cream
- 1 cup shredded part-skim mozzarella cheese
- 1 cup chopped Mustard Pork Tenderloin (below)
- 1 avocado, chopped
- 1 jalapeño pepper, minced
- 10 (6-inch) corn tortillas
- 2 tablespoons olive oil

Directions:
1. In medium bowl, combine sour cream, cheese, pork tenderloin, avocado, and jalapeño pepper and mix gently.
2. Divide mixture among half the tortillas, placing the remaining half of tortillas on top to make sandwiches. Heat griddle and brush with olive oil. Place quesadillas on the griddle; cover and grill for 2–3 minutes on each side until tortillas are crisp and cheese is melted. Cut into quarters and serve.

Nutrition Info:
- Info Per Serving: Calories: 315.36 ; Fat:16.67 g ;Saturated fat:5.55 g ;Sodium:161.17 mg

Sirloin Steak With Root Vegetables

Servings: X
Cooking Time: 40 Minutes
Ingredients:
- 1 (10-ounce) sirloin steak, fat trimmed
- Sea salt
- Freshly ground black pepper
- 2 carrots, cut into 1-inch chunks
- 2 parsnip, cut into 1-inch chunks
- 1 small celeriac, peeled and cut into 1-inch chunks
- 1 small sweet potato, peeled and cut into 1-inch chunks
- 6 beets, peeled and halved
- 1 tablespoon olive oil, plus extra for drizzling

Directions:
1. Preheat the oven to 400°F.
2. Line a sheet pan with foil and set aside.
3. Season the steak with salt and pepper and set aside.
4. Spread the veggies on the sheet pan, leaving room for the steak. Season them lightly with salt and pepper and drizzle with 1 tablespoon olive oil.
5. Roast the veggies until they are lightly caramelized and tender, about 30 minutes.
6. Remove the sheet pan from the oven and add the steak.
7. Increase the oven temperature to broil.

8. Place the sheet pan into the oven and broil until the steak is browned, 4 to 5 minutes per side for medium-rare, or until it reaches your desired doneness.
9. Serve.

Nutrition Info:
- Info Per Serving: Calories: 565 ; Fat: 26 g ;Saturated fat: 8 g ;Sodium: 274 mg

Wasabi-roasted Filet Mignon

Servings: 12
Cooking Time: X
Ingredients:
- 1 (3-pound) filet mignon roast
- ¼ teaspoon pepper
- 1 teaspoon powdered wasabi
- 2 tablespoons sesame oil
- 2 tablespoons soy sauce

Directions:
1. Preheat oven to 400ºF. If the roast has a thin end and a thick end, fold the thin end under so the roast is about the same thickness. Place on roasting pan.
2. In small bowl, combine pepper, wasabi, oil, and soy sauce, and mix well. Brush half over roast. Roast the beef for 30 minutes, then remove and brush with remaining wasabi mixture. Return to oven for 5–10 minutes longer or until meat thermometer registers at least 145ºF for medium rare.
3. Remove from oven, cover, and let stand for 15 minutes before slicing to serve.

Nutrition Info:
- Info Per Serving: Calories:298.15; Fat: 24.00g ;Saturated fat:8.99 g ;Sodium: 143.07 mg

Beef And Broccoli

Servings: 4
Cooking Time: 10 Minutes
Ingredients:
- ½ pound top sirloin steak
- ⅛ teaspoon cayenne pepper
- ¼ teaspoon ground ginger
- 1¼ cups low-sodium beef broth
- 1 tablespoon honey
- 2 tablespoons cornstarch
- 1 teaspoon hoisin sauce
- 1 teaspoon low-sodium soy sauce
- 1 teaspoon olive oil
- 1 onion, chopped
- 3 cloves garlic, minced
- 3 cups broccoli florets

Directions:

1. Trim any visible fat from the steak. Cut the steak into ½-inch strips. Place in a bowl, sprinkle with the cayenne pepper and ginger, and toss. Set aside.

2. In a small bowl, thoroughly combine the beef broth, honey, cornstarch, hoisin sauce, and soy sauce. Set aside.

3. In a large nonstick skillet or wok, heat the olive oil over medium-high heat.

4. Add the steak strips in a single layer, and cook for 1 minute. Turn the steak and cook for 1 minute longer. Transfer the steak to a plate.

5. Add the onion and garlic to the skillet, and stir-fry for 2 minutes.

6. Add the broccoli, and stir-fry for 2 minutes.

7. Add the broth mixture and bring to a simmer. Simmer for 1 to 2 minutes or until the sauce has thickened.

8. Return the beef to the skillet, and stir-fry for 1 minute. Serve immediately.

Nutrition Info:

*   Info Per Serving: Calories: 204 ; Fat:9 g ;Saturated fat: 3g ;Sodium: 141 mg

Spicy Rib Eye In Red Sauce

Servings: 6
Cooking Time: X
Ingredients:

*   1¼ pounds rib eye steak
*   1/8 teaspoon salt
*   1/8 teaspoon cayenne pepper
*   1 tablespoon olive oil
*   1 onion, chopped
*   3 cloves garlic, minced
*   1/3 cup dry red wine
*   1 tablespoon chili powder
*   ½ teaspoon crushed red pepper flakes
*   ½ teaspoon coriander seed
*   1 (20-ounce) can no-salt crushed tomatoes

Directions:

1. Trim excess fat from steak and sprinkle with salt and pepper. Heat a skillet over medium-high heat and add olive oil. Add steak to pan; cook without moving until steak is browned, about 4–6 minutes. Turn steak and cook for 2–3 minutes on second side, until medium rare. Remove to plate.

2. Add onion and garlic to drippings remaining in skillet. Cook and stir until tender, about 4 minutes. Add wine, chili powder, red pepper flakes, coriander, and tomatoes and bring to a simmer. Reduce heat to low and simmer for 15 minutes until sauce is reduced and thickened.

3. Thinly slice the steak against the grain and add to the sauce. Cook and stir for 2–3 minutes or until steak is hot and tender and sauce is blended. Serve immediately over brown rice, couscous, quinoa, or pasta.

Nutrition Info:

*   Info Per Serving: Calories:267.81; Fat:10.22 g ;Saturated fat:3.27 g;Sodium:138.71 mg

Risotto With Ham And Pineapple

Servings: 4–6
Cooking Time: X
Ingredients:

*   2 cups water
*   2 cups Low-Fat Chicken Broth
*   1 tablespoon olive oil
*   1 tablespoon butter
*   1 onion, chopped
*   3 cloves garlic, minced
*   ½ teaspoon dried thyme leaves
*   1 red bell pepper, chopped
*   1½ cups Arborio rice
*   1 cup chopped ham
*   1 (20-ounce) can pineapple tidbits, drained
*   1/8 teaspoon pepper
*   ¼ cup grated Parmesan cheese

Directions:

1. In medium saucepan, combine water and chicken broth and bring to a simmer over low heat. Keep warm. In large saucepan, heat olive oil and butter over medium heat. Add onion and garlic; cook and stir for 3 minutes. Add thyme, bell pepper, and rice; cook and stir for 4 minutes.

2. Start adding the broth, 1 cup at a time, stirring frequently. When 1 cup broth remains to be added, add ham, pineapple, and pepper to risotto. Add last cup of broth; cook and stir until rice is tender and creamy and liquid is absorbed. Stir in Parmesan, cover, let stand for 5 minutes, then serve.

Nutrition Info:

*   Info Per Serving: Calories:369.77; Fat: 8.92 g ;Saturated fat: 3.17 g ;Sodium: 390.26 mg

Dark Beer Beef Chili

Servings: X
Cooking Time: 50 Minutes
Ingredients:

*   1 teaspoon olive oil
*   6 ounces extra-lean ground beef
*   ½ sweet onion, chopped
*   1 green bell pepper, diced
*   1 teaspoon minced garlic
*   2 cups low-sodium canned diced tomatoes, with their juices
*   ½ cup low-sodium canned kidney beans, rinsed and drained
*   ½ cup low-sodium canned lentils, rinsed and drained
*   ½ cup dark beer
*   1 tablespoon chili powder
*   ½ teaspoon ground cumin
*   Pinch cayenne powder
*   2 teaspoons chopped fresh cilantro, for garnish
*   4 tablespoons fat-free sour cream, for garnish

Directions:

1. In a large saucepan, warm the oil over medium-high heat.
2. Add the ground beef and cook until browned, about 5 minutes.
3. Add the onions, bell pepper, and garlic and sauté until softened, about 4 minutes.
4. Stir in the tomatoes, kidney beans, lentils, beer, chili powder, cumin, and cayenne powder.
5. Bring the mixture to a boil and then reduce the heat. Simmer, partially covered, until the flavors come together and the liquid is almost gone, 35 to 40 minutes.
6. Serve topped with cilantro and sour cream.

Nutrition Info:

- Info Per Serving: Calories: 415 ; Fat: 10 g ;Saturated fat: 2 g ;Sodium: 125 mg

Fruit-stuffed Pork Tenderloin

Servings: 6
Cooking Time: X

Ingredients:

- 1½ pounds pork tenderloin
- ¼ cup dry white wine
- 6 prunes, chopped
- 5 dried apricots, chopped
- 1 onion, chopped
- 2 tablespoons flour
- 1/8 teaspoon salt
- 1/8 teaspoon pepper
- 2 tablespoons olive oil
- ½ cup Low-Sodium Chicken Broth
- 1 teaspoon dried thyme leaves

Directions:

1. Trim excess fat from meat. Cut tenderloin lengthwise, cutting to, but not through, the other side. Open up the meat and place on work surface, cut side up. Lightly pound with a rolling pin or meat mallet until about ½" thick.
2. In small saucepan, combine wine, prunes, apricots, and onion. Simmer for 10 minutes or until fruit is soft and wine is absorbed. Place this mixture in the center of the pork tenderloin. Roll the pork around the fruit mixture, using a toothpick to secure.
3. Sprinkle pork with flour, salt, and pepper. In ovenproof saucepan, heat olive oil. Add pork; brown on all sides, turning frequently, about 5–6 minutes. Add broth and thyme to saucepan. Bake for 25–35 minutes or until internal temperature registers 155ºF. Let pork stand for 5 minutes, remove toothpicks, and slice to serve.

Nutrition Info:

- Info Per Serving: Calories: 249.06 ; Fat: 9.82 g ;Saturated fat: 2.41 g ;Sodium: 102.85 mg

Canadian-bacon Risotto

Servings: 6
Cooking Time: X

Ingredients:

- 2 cups water
- 3 cups Low-Sodium Chicken Broth
- 1 tablespoon olive oil
- 1 chopped onion
- 3 cloves garlic, minced
- 1 (8-ounce) package sliced mushrooms
- ½ teaspoon dried oregano leaves
- 1 teaspoon dried basil leaves
- 2 cups Arborio rice
- 1/8 teaspoon white pepper
- 1 cup chopped Canadian bacon
- ¼ cup shredded Parmesan cheese
- 1 tablespoon butter

Directions:

1. In medium saucepan, combine water and broth; heat over low heat until warm; keep on heat.
2. In large saucepan, heat olive oil over medium heat. Add onion, garlic, and mushrooms to pan; cook and stir until crisp-tender, about 4 minutes. Add oregano and basil.
3. Add rice; cook and stir for 2 minutes. Add the broth mixture, a cup at a time, stirring until the liquid is absorbed, about 15 minutes. When there is 1 cup broth remaining, add pepper and Canadian bacon along with the last cup of broth. Cook and stir until rice is tender, about 5 minutes.
4. Stir in Parmesan and butter and serve immediately.

Nutrition Info:

- Info Per Serving: Calories: 379.72; Fat: 9.41 g ;Saturated fat:3.17g ;Sodium: 292.55 mg

Herb-crusted Pork Tenderloin

Servings: 8
Cooking Time: X

Ingredients:

- 1/3 cup chopped flat-leaf parsley
- 4 fresh sage leaves, chopped
- ¼ cup dried breadcrumbs
- 2 tablespoons fresh thyme leaves
- 1 tablespoon mustard
- 1 tablespoon olive oil
- 2 (1-pound) pork tenderloins
- 1/8 teaspoon salt
- 1/8 teaspoon pepper
- 2 tablespoons olive oil

Directions:

1. Preheat oven to 400ºF. On shallow plate, combine parsley, sage, breadcrumbs, and thyme leaves and mix until combined. Add mustard and olive oil; toss until combined. Set aside.

2. Sprinkle tenderloins with salt and pepper. Heat 2 tablespoons olive oil in heavy ovenproof saucepan over medium high heat. Sear tenderloins on all sides, about 2 minutes a side, until golden brown.

3. Remove pan from heat. Carefully press herb mixture onto top and sides of tenderloins. Roast for 15–20 minutes or until internal temperature registers 155ºF. Let pork stand for 5 minutes, then serve.

Nutrition Info:

- Info Per Serving: Calories:199.58; Fat: 9.77 g ;Saturated fat :2.63 g ;Sodium: 139.95 mg

Spinach And Kale Salad With Spicy Pork

Servings: 4
Cooking Time: 10 Minutes
Ingredients:

- 1 tablespoon olive oil, divided
- 2 tablespoons buttermilk
- 2 tablespoons lime juice
- 2 tablespoons low-sodium yellow mustard
- ½ teaspoon fennel seed
- 1 pound plain pork tenderloin
- Pinch salt
- ⅛ teaspoon cayenne pepper
- 2 teaspoons chili powder
- 3 cups baby spinach leaves, rinsed and dried
- 2 cups torn kale leaves, rinsed and dried, stem removed
- 1 carrot, shredded
- 1 red bell pepper, seeded and chopped
- 1 tablespoon crumbled soft goat cheese

Directions:

1. In a small bowl, make the dressing: Combine 2 teaspoons of the olive oil, the buttermilk, lime juice, mustard, and fennel seed, and mix well with a whisk until combined. Set aside.

2. Slice the pork tenderloin into 1-inch pieces and put into a medium bowl. Sprinkle with the salt, cayenne pepper, and chili powder.

3. Heat the remaining 1 teaspoon olive oil in a large nonstick skillet. Add the tenderloin pieces, cut side down. Cook for 4 minutes without turning.

4. Turn the pork and cook for 2 to 3 minutes or until the pork registers 150°F on a meat thermometer. Remove from the pan to a clean plate and cover with an aluminum foil tent to keep warm.

5. In a large salad bowl, toss the spinach, kale, carrot, and bell pepper. Add the salad dressing and toss to coat. Top with the pork and goat cheese, and serve immediately.

Nutrition Info:

- Info Per Serving: Calories: 207 ; Fat: 9 g ;Saturated fat: 2 g ;Sodium: 213 mg

Beef Risotto

Servings: 6
Cooking Time: X
Ingredients:

- 2 cups water
- 2 cups Low-Sodium Beef Broth
- 2 tablespoons olive oil
- ½ pound sirloin steak, chopped
- 1 onion, minced 2 cloves garlic, minced
- 1½ cups Arborio rice
- 2 tablespoons steak sauce
- ¼ teaspoon pepper
- 1 pound asparagus, cut into 2″ pieces
- ¼ cup grated Parmesan cheese
- 1 tablespoon butter

Directions:

1. In medium saucepan, combine water and broth; heat over low heat until warm; keep on heat.

2. In large saucepan, heat olive oil over medium heat. Add beef; cook and stir until browned. Remove from pan with slotted spoon and set aside. Add onion and garlic to pan; cook and stir until crisp-tender, about 4 minutes.

3. Add rice; cook and stir for 2 minutes. Add the broth mixture, a cup at a time, stirring until the liquid is absorbed, about 15 minutes. When there is 1 cup broth remaining, return the beef to the pot and add the steak sauce, pepper, and asparagus. Cook and stir until rice is tender, beef is cooked, and asparagus is tender, about 5 minutes. Stir in Parmesan and butter and serve immediately.

Nutrition Info:

- Info Per Serving: Calories: 365.04; Fat: 11.67 g ;Saturated fat: 4.09 g ;Sodium: 138.81 mg

Maple-balsamic Pork Chops

Servings: X
Cooking Time: 20 Minutes
Ingredients:

- ¼ cup low-sodium chicken broth
- 2 tablespoons maple syrup
- 1 tablespoon balsamic vinegar
- ¼ teaspoon chopped fresh thyme
- 2 (4-ounce) boneless pork top-loin chops
- Sea salt
- Freshly ground black pepper
- Nonstick olive oil cooking spray

Directions:

1. In a small bowl, stir together the chicken broth, maple syrup, vinegar, and thyme.

2. Season the pork chops on both sides with sea salt and pepper.

3. Place a medium skillet over medium-high heat and spray generously with cooking spray. Add the pork chops and cook, about 6 minutes on each side.

4. Add the sauce to the skillet and turn the chops to coat completely.

5. Continue to cook until the pork chops are cooked through, about 6 minutes more, turning once.

6. Let the pork rest for 10 minutes and serve.

Nutrition Info:

- Info Per Serving: Calories:163 ; Fat: 7 g ;Saturated fat: 2 g ;Sodium: 212 mg

Pork Scallops With Spinach

Servings: 6
Cooking Time: X

Ingredients:

- 3 tablespoons flour
- 1/8 teaspoon salt
- 1/8 teaspoon pepper
- 6 (3-ounce) pork scallops
- 2 tablespoons olive oil
- 1 onion, chopped
- 1 (10-ounce) package frozen chopped spinach, thawed
- 1 tablespoon flour
- ½ teaspoon celery seed
- 1/3 cup nonfat light cream
- 1/3 cup part-skim ricotta cheese
- ½ cup dried breadcrumbs, divided
- 2 tablespoons grated Romano cheese

Directions:

1. Preheat oven to 350ºF. On plate, combine 3 tablespoons flour, salt, and pepper and mix well. Pound pork scallops, if necessary, to A1/8" thickness.

2. Heat olive oil in nonstick pan over medium-high heat. Dredge pork in flour mixture and sauté in pan, turning once, until just browned, about 1 minute per side. Remove to a baking dish.

3. Add onion to pan; cook and stir for 3 minutes. Drain spinach well and add to pan; cook and stir until liquid evaporates. Add flour and celery seed; cook and stir for 1 minute.

4. Stir in light cream; cook and stir until thickened, about 3 minutes. Remove from heat and add ricotta cheese and half of the breadcrumbs.

5. Divide spinach mixture on top of pork in baking dish. Top with remaining breadcrumbs and Romano. Bake for 10–15 minutes or until pork is tender and thoroughly cooked. Serve immediately.

Nutrition Info:

- Info Per Serving: Calories: 298.66; Fat: 12.60 g ;Saturated fat:4.08 g ;Sodium: 303.25 mg

Pork Tenderloin With Apples

Servings: 6
Cooking Time: X

Ingredients:

- 1½ pounds pork tenderloin
- 1/8 teaspoon salt
- 1/8 teaspoon pepper
- 2 tablespoons flour
- 2 tablespoons olive oil
- 1 onion, chopped
- 4 cloves garlic, minced
- 2 apples, thinly sliced
- ½ cup dry white wine
- 1 tablespoon chopped fresh rosemary

Directions:

1. Trim excess fat from pork and sprinkle with salt, pepper, and flour. Heat olive oil in large saucepan and brown pork on all sides, about 5 minutes total.

2. Add onion, garlic, apples, and wine to saucepan, and bring to a simmer. Reduce heat to low, cover, and simmer for 20 minutes. Add rosemary, uncover, and simmer for 5–10 minutes longer or until pork registers 155ºF. Let stand for 5 minutes off the heat, then serve.

Nutrition Info:

- Info Per Serving: Calories: 243.96 ; Fat:9.42 g ;Saturated fat: 2.34 g ;Sodium: 100.07 mg

Steak-and-pepper Kabobs

Servings: 4
Cooking Time: X

Ingredients:

- 2 tablespoons brown sugar
- ½ teaspoon garlic powder
- 1/8 teaspoon cayenne pepper
- ¼ teaspoon onion salt
- ½ teaspoon chili powder
- 1/8 teaspoon ground cloves
- 1 (1-pound) sirloin steak, cut in
- 1″ cubes
- 2 red bell peppers, cut in strips
- 2 green bell peppers, cut in strips

Directions:

1. In small bowl, combine brown sugar, garlic powder, cayenne pepper, onion salt, chili powder, and clove, and mix well. Toss sirloin steak with brown sugar mixture. Place in glass dish and cover; refrigerate for 2 hours.

2. When ready to cook, prepare and preheat grill. Thread steak cubes and pepper strips on metal skewers. Grill 6″ from medium coals for 5–8 minutes, turning once, until steak reaches desired doneness and peppers are crisp-tender. Serve immediately.

Nutrition Info:

- Info Per Serving: Calories: 205.53; Fat: 6.23 g ;Saturated fat: 2.24 g ;Sodium: 133.03 mg

Prosciutto Fruit Omelet

Servings: 4
Cooking Time: X
Ingredients:
- ¼ pound thinly sliced prosciutto
- ½ cup shredded part-skim mozzarella cheese
- 2 tablespoons grated Parmesan cheese
- 1 egg
- 8 egg whites
- ¼ cup low-fat sour cream
- 1/8 teaspoon pepper
- 1 tablespoon olive oil
- 1 apple, chopped

Directions:
1. Trim off excess fat from prosciutto and discard. Thinly slice the pro-sciutto and combine with the mozzarella and Parmesan cheeses. Set aside.
2. In large bowl, combine egg, egg whites, sour cream, and pepper and mix well. In large nonstick saucepan, heat olive oil over medium heat; add apples and stir until apples are tender. Pour in egg mixture.
3. Cook, running spatula around edges to let uncooked mixture flow underneath, until eggs are almost set and bottom is golden brown.
4. Sprinkle with cheese and ham mixture and cook for 2–3 minutes longer. Cover, remove from heat, and let stand for 2 minutes. Fold omelet over on itself and slide onto plate to serve.

Nutrition Info:
- Info Per Serving: Calories:221.48; Fat:12.35 g ;Saturated fat:4.99 g ;Sodium: 551.41 mg

Sirloin Meatballs In Sauce

Servings: 6
Cooking Time: X
Ingredients:
- 1 tablespoon olive oil
- 3 cloves garlic, minced
- ½ cup minced onion
- 2 egg whites
- ½ cup dry breadcrumbs
- ¼ cup grated Parmesan cheese
- ½ teaspoon crushed fennel seeds
- ½ teaspoon dried oregano leaves
- 2 teaspoons Worcestershire sauce
- 1/8 teaspoon pepper
- 1/8 teaspoon crushed red pepper flakes
- 1 pound 95% lean ground sirloin
- 1 recipe Spaghetti Sauce

Directions:

1. In small saucepan, heat olive oil over medium heat. Add garlic and onion; cook and stir until tender, about 5 minutes. Remove from heat and place in large mixing bowl.
2. Add egg whites, breadcrumbs, Parmesan, fennel, oregano, Worcestershire sauce, pepper, and pepper flakes and mix well. Add sirloin; mix gently but thoroughly until combined. Form into 12 meatballs.
3. In large nonstick saucepan, place Spaghetti Sauce and bring to a simmer. Carefully add meatballs to sauce. Return to a simmer, partially cover, and simmer for 15–25 minutes or until meatballs are thoroughly cooked.

Nutrition Info:
- Info Per Serving: Calories: 367.93; Fat: 13.56 g ;Saturated fat: 3.91 g;Sodium: 305.47 mg

Beef And Avocado Quesadillas

Servings: 4
Cooking Time: 10 Minutes
Ingredients:
- ½ pound 98% lean ground beef
- 1 small onion, chopped
- 3 cloves garlic, minced
- 8 medium mushrooms, sliced
- 1 cup shredded carrot
- ½ cup low-sodium salsa
- ½ cup low-fat mozzarella cheese
- ½ avocado, peeled and diced
- 4 whole-wheat flour tortillas

Directions:
1. In a large nonstick skillet, sauté the ground beef, onion, garlic, mushrooms, and carrot, stirring to break up the meat, until the meat is browned and fully cooked, about 5 to 6 minutes. Drain if necessary.
2. Transfer the beef mixture to a medium bowl and stir in the salsa.
3. Place the tortillas on the work surface. Divide the meat mixture among them, placing the meat on half of the tortilla. Top with the cheese and avocado. Fold the tortillas over and press gently into a quesadilla.
4. Rinse and dry the nonstick skillet.
5. One at a time, place the quesadillas into the skillet over medium heat, and cook for 2 to 3 minutes on each side. Cut the quesadillas in half and serve immediately.

Nutrition Info:
- Info Per Serving: Calories: 237 ; Fat: 9 g ;Saturated fat: 3 g ;Sodium: 344 mg

Beef-and-pumpkin Quinoa Pilaf

Servings: 6
Cooking Time: X
Ingredients:

- 1 tablespoon olive oil
- 1 pound sirloin steak, cubed
- 1 onion, chopped
- 1 cup quinoa
- 2½ cups Low-Sodium Beef Broth
- 1 cup canned solid-pack pumpkin
- ¼ cup grated Parmesan cheese
- ½ cup chopped flat-leaf parsley
- 4 chopped fresh sage leaves
- 1/8 teaspoon nutmeg
- ½ cup toasted no-salt pumpkin seeds

Directions:

1. In large saucepan, heat olive oil over medium heat. Add steak; cook and stir until browned, about 5 minutes. Add onion; cook and stir for 3 minutes longer. Add quinoa and stir.

2. Pour in the beef broth; bring to a simmer. Cover and simmer for 10 minutes. Then add pumpkin; cook and stir until hot, about 4 minutes. Stir in Parmesan, parsley, sage leaves, and nutmeg. Stir, pour into serving dish, and top with pumpkin seeds. Serve immediately.

Nutrition Info:

- Info Per Serving: Calories: 317.83 ; Fat:10.72g ;Saturated fat: 3.21 g;Sodium:119.79 mg

Stuffed Meatloaf

Servings: 8
Cooking Time: X
Ingredients:

- 1 tablespoon butter
- 1 onion, chopped
- 1 (8-ounce) package sliced mushrooms
- ½ (10-ounce) package frozen spinach, thawed and drained
- 2 tablespoons chopped fresh parsley
- 1 recipe Whole-Grain Meatloaf , uncooked
- 2 tablespoons ketchup
- 2 tablespoons mustard

Directions:

1. Preheat oven to 350ºF. Spray a 9″ × 5″ loaf pan with nonstick cooking spray and set aside. In medium saucepan, melt butter over medium heat. Add onion and mushrooms; cook and stir for 3 minutes. Then add spinach; cook until the vegetables are tender and the liquid evaporates.

2. Remove from heat and stir in parsley. Press half of the meatloaf mixture into prepared pan. Top with mushroom mixture, keeping mixture away from sides of pan. Top with remaining meatloaf mixture.

3. In small bowl, combine ketchup and mustard and mix well. Spoon over meatloaf. Bake for 55–65 minutes or until internal temperature registers 165ºF. Let stand for 10 minutes, then cut into slices.

Nutrition Info:

- Info Per Serving: Calories:362.10 ; Fat: 17.28 g ;Saturated fat:5.65 g ;Sodium: 258.17 mg

Chile Pork With Soba Noodles

Servings: 4
Cooking Time: 15 Minutes
Ingredients:

- 3 (4-ounce) boneless top loin pork chops
- Pinch salt
- 2 teaspoons chili powder
- ⅛ teaspoon cayenne pepper
- 1 cup low-sodium chicken broth
- 1 tablespoon rice wine vinegar
- 1 teaspoon low-sodium soy sauce
- 1 tablespoon cornstarch
- 8 ounces soba noodles
- 1 teaspoon toasted sesame oil
- 1 carrot, grated
- 1 red chile pepper, seeded and minced
- 2 scallions, chopped
- 1 small zucchini, sliced

Directions:

1. Bring a large pot of water to a boil.

2. Trim excess fat from the pork chops and discard. Cut the chops into 1-inch cubes, and put them in a medium bowl. Toss with the salt, chili powder, and cayenne pepper, and set aside.

3. In a small bowl, combine the chicken broth, rice wine vinegar, soy sauce, and cornstarch, and set aside.

4. Cook the soba noodles according to the package directions, about 6 minutes. Drain in a colander, rinse with cool water, and set aside.

5. In a large nonstick skillet or wok over medium-high heat, heat the sesame oil. Add the pork pieces and stir-fry 3 to 4 minutes or until the pork is almost cooked. Transfer to a clean plate.

6. Add the carrot, chile pepper, scallions, and zucchini to the skillet; stir-fry for 3 to 4 minutes or until crisp-tender.

7. Add the chicken broth mixture, the pork, and the soba noodles to the skillet, and stir-fry 2 to 3 minutes or until the sauce simmers and is thickened. Serve immediately.

Nutrition Info:

- Info Per Serving: Calories: 342 ; Fat: 5 g ;Saturated fat: 2 g ;Sodium: 542 mg

Thin Pork Chops With Mushrooms And Herbs

Servings: 4
Cooking Time: X
Ingredients:

- 3 tablespoons flour
- ¼ teaspoon salt
- 1/8 teaspoon white pepper
- 1 teaspoon dried thyme leaves
- 4 (3-ounce) boneless pork chops
- 2 tablespoons olive oil
- 2 shallots, minced
- 1 cup sliced cremini mushrooms
- 1 tablespoon fresh rosemary leaves, minced
- ¼ cup dry sherry

Directions:

1. On shallow plate, combine flour, salt, pepper, and thyme leaves and mix well. Place pork between two sheets of waxed paper and pound until ½" thick. Dredge pork chops in mixture, shaking off excess.

2. Heat olive oil in large skillet over medium heat. Add pork chops; brown on first side without moving, about 4 minutes.

3. Turn pork and add shallots and mushrooms to the pan. Cook for 3 minutes, then remove pork from pan. Stir vegetables, scraping pan to remove drippings.

4. Add rosemary and sherry to pan and bring to a boil. Return pork to skillet, lower heat, and simmer pork for 2–4 minutes longer until pork is very light pink. Serve immediately.

Nutrition Info:

- Info Per Serving: Calories:238.91 ; Fat:14.92 g ;Saturated fat: 3.97 g ;Sodium:392.89 mg

Mini Lasagna Cups

Servings: 3
Cooking Time: 18 Minutes
Ingredients:

- ⅓ pound 98% lean ground beef
- 2 scallions, minced
- 3 cloves garlic, minced
- 1¼ cups low-sodium marinara sauce
- 1 teaspoon dried Italian seasoning
- ¾ cup low-fat ricotta cheese
- ¼ cup grated Romano cheese
- 6 (4-inch) corn tortillas

Directions:

1. Preheat the oven to 375°F. Spray 6 standard muffin cups with nonstick cooking spray and set aside.

2. In a medium nonstick skillet, sauté the ground beef with the scallions and garlic over medium-high heat, stirring to break up the meat, until the beef is browned, about 3 minutes. Drain if necessary.

3. Stir the marinara sauce and Italian seasoning into the beef mixture. Remove from the heat, then cut the corn tortillas into thirds.

4. Dip a piece of tortilla into the meat sauce and put it into a muffin cup. Top with 2 tablespoons meat sauce. Top with one corn tortilla piece. Top with two tablespoons ricotta cheese. Add another tortilla piece, then 2 tablespoons meat sauce. Sprinkle with the Romano cheese. Repeat, filling the remaining 5 muffin cups.

5. Bake the lasagna cups for 10 to 15 minutes or until the cups are bubbling and the cheese on top is lightly browned. Transfer the muffin tin to a cooling rack.

6. Let stand for 5 minutes, then run a knife around the edges of each muffin cup and remove the mini lasagnas.

Nutrition Info:

- Info Per Serving: Calories: 266 ; Fat: 10 g ;Saturated fat: 4 g ;Sodium: 357 mg

Pork Chops With Cabbage

Servings: 6
Cooking Time: X
Ingredients:

- 1 red onion, chopped
- 4 cloves garlic, minced
- 3 cups chopped red cabbage
- 3 cups chopped green cabbage
- 1 apple, chopped
- 6 (3-ounce) boneless pork chops
- 1/8 teaspoon white pepper
- 1 tablespoon olive oil
- ¼ cup brown sugar
- ¼ cup apple cider vinegar
- 1 tablespoon mustard

Directions:

1. In 4- to 5-quart slow cooker, combine onion, garlic, cabbages, and apple and mix well.

2. Trim pork chops of any excess fat and sprinkle with pepper. Heat olive oil in large saucepan over medium heat. Brown chops on just one side, about 3 minutes. Add to slow cooker with vegetables.

3. In small bowl, combine brown sugar, vinegar, and mustard and mix well. Pour into slow cooker. Cover and cook on low for 7–8 hours or until pork and cabbage are tender. Serve immediately.

Nutrition Info:

- Info Per Serving: Calories: 242.86 ; Fat: 10.57 g ;Saturated fat:3.37 g ;Sodium:364.80 mg

Beef Rollups With Pesto

Servings: 6
Cooking Time: X
Ingredients:

- ½ cup packed basil leaves
- ½ cup packed baby spinach leaves
- 3 cloves garlic, minced
- 1/3 cup toasted chopped hazelnuts
- 1/8 teaspoon white pepper
- 2 tablespoons grated Parmesan cheese
- 2 tablespoons olive oil
- 2 tablespoons water
- 3 tablespoons flour
- ½ teaspoon paprika
- 6 (4-ounce) top round steaks, ¼″ thick
- 2 oil-packed sun-dried tomatoes, minced
- 1 tablespoon canola oil
- 1 cup Low-Sodium Beef Broth

Directions:

1. In blender or food processor, combine basil, spinach, garlic, hazelnuts, and white pepper, and blend or process until finely chopped. Add Parmesan and blend again. Add olive oil and blend until a paste forms, then add water and blend.
2. On shallow plate, combine flour, and paprika and mix well. Place beef between sheets of waxed paper and pound until A″ thick. Spread pesto on one side of the pounded beef and sprinkle with tomatoes. Roll up, fastening closed with toothpicks.
3. Dredge rollups in flour mixture. Heat canola oil in large saucepan and brown rollups on all sides, about 5 minutes total. Pour beef broth into pan and bring to a simmer. Cover, reduce heat to low, and simmer for 40–50 minutes or until beef is tender.

Nutrition Info:

- Info Per Serving: Calories: 290.23 ; Fat:18.73g ;Saturated fat:3.90 g ;Sodium:95.79 mg

Mustard And Thyme–crusted Beef Tenderloin

Servings: X
Cooking Time: 15 Minutes
Ingredients:

- ¼ cup grainy mustard
- 1 tablespoon chopped fresh thyme
- 1 teaspoon chopped fresh parsley
- 2 (3-ounce) beef tenderloin steaks, fat trimmed
- Sea salt
- Freshly ground black pepper
- Nonstick olive oil cooking spray

Directions:

1. Preheat the oven for 400°F.

2. In a small bowl, stir together the mustard, thyme, and parsley until well blended.
3. Lightly season the beef with salt and pepper.
4. Coat a medium oven-safe skillet with cooking spray and place over medium-high heat.
5. Add the beef and cook until browned on both sides, about 4 minutes per side.
6. Remove the skillet from the heat and spread the mustard mixture all over each steak.
7. Place the skillet in the oven and roast the beef until desired doneness, about 8 minutes for medium.
8. Let the meat rest for 10 minutes and serve.

Nutrition Info:

- Info Per Serving: Calories: 224 ; Fat: 11 g ;Saturated fat: 5 g ;Sodium: 206 mg

Whole-grain Meatloaf

Servings: 8
Cooking Time: X
Ingredients:

- 1 tablespoon olive oil
- 1 onion, finely chopped
- 3 cloves garlic, minced
- 1 cup minced mushrooms
- 1/8 teaspoon pepper
- 1 teaspoon dried marjoram leaves
- 1 egg
- 1 egg white
- ½ cup chili sauce
- ¼ cup milk
- 1 tablespoon Worcestershire sauce
- 4 slices Whole-Grain Oatmeal Bread
- 8 ounces 85% lean ground beef
- 8 ounces ground turkey
- 8 ounces ground pork
- 3 tablespoons ketchup

Directions:

1. Preheat oven to 325°F. Spray a 9″ × 5″ loaf pan with nonstick cooking spray and set aside. In large saucepan, heat olive oil over medium heat. Add onion, garlic, and mushrooms; cook and stir until tender, about 6 minutes. Place in large mixing bowl, sprinkle with pepper and marjoram, and let stand for 15 minutes.
2. Add egg, egg white, chili sauce, milk, and Worcestershire sauce, and mix well. Make crumbs from the oatmeal bread and add to onion mixture.
3. Add all of the meat and work gently with your hands just until combined. Press into prepared loaf pan. Top with ketchup. Bake for 60–75 minutes, or until internal temperature registers 165°F. Remove from oven, cover with foil, and let stand for 10 minutes before slicing.

Nutrition Info:

- Info Per Serving: Calories: 325.29; Fat:15.51 g ;Saturated fat:4.70 g;Sodium: 184.45 mg

Pork Loin With Cranberry Bbq Sauce

Servings: 12
Cooking Time: X
Ingredients:
- 1 (3-pound) lean pork loin roast
- ¼ cup low-sodium ketchup
- 3 tablespoons apple cider vinegar
- 3 tablespoons spicy brown mustard
- 2 tablespoons brown sugar
- 3 cloves garlic
- 1 onion, minced
- ½ cup chopped fresh cranberries
- ¼ cup water
- 1/8 teaspoon pepper

Directions:
1. Preheat oven to 350ºF. Trim excess fat from pork roast and place in roasting pan. Roast for 45 minutes.
2. Meanwhile, combine ketchup, vinegar, mustard, brown sugar, garlic, onion, cranberries, water, and pepper in small saucepan and bring to a boil. Simmer for 5 minutes, then remove from heat.
3. Remove pork from oven and baste with sauce. Continue roasting, basting every 5 minutes with sauce, for another 40–50 minutes or until pork registers 155ºF on a meat thermometer. Let rest for 5 minutes.
4. While pork is resting, simmer remaining sauce for 2 minutes. Slice pork and serve with sauce.

Nutrition Info:
- Info Per Serving: Calories: 275.13; Fat:12.34 g ;Saturated fat: 4.45 g ;Sodium: 95.07 mg

Cabbage Roll Sauté

Servings: X
Cooking Time: 30 Minutes
Ingredients:
- 4 cups water
- ½ cup brown rice, rinsed
- Nonstick olive oil cooking spray
- 6 ounces extra-lean ground beef
- ¼ small sweet onion, chopped
- ½ teaspoon minced garlic
- 2 cups crushed tomatoes
- 1 tablespoon brown sugar
- 2 teaspoons balsamic vinegar
- ¼ teaspoon paprika
- 2 cups thinly shredded cabbage
- 2 teaspoons chopped fresh parsley, for garnish

Directions:
1. Warm the water in a medium saucepan over high heat and bring to a boil.
2. Add the rice and reduce the heat to medium-low. Simmer until the rice is tender, about 30 minutes.
3. Drain any excess water and set the rice aside, covered, to keep warm.
4. Generously coat a large skillet with cooking spray and place over medium-high heat.
5. Add the beef and cook until browned, breaking it up, 5 to 7 minutes.
6. Stir in the onion and garlic and sauté until the vegetables are softened, about 3 minutes.
7. Stir in the crushed tomatoes, sugar, vinegar, and paprika and bring the sauce to a boil.
8. Stir in the cabbage and reduce the heat to low. Simmer until the cabbage is very tender, 10 to 12 minutes.
9. Serve the cabbage roll mixture over the rice, topped with parsley.

Nutrition Info:
- Info Per Serving: Calories: 473 ; Fat: 9 g ;Saturated fat: 3 g ;Sodium: 328 mg

Fish And Seafood

Fennel-grilled Haddock

Servings: 4
Cooking Time: X
Ingredients:

- 2 bulbs fennel
- 4 (5-ounce) haddock or halibut steaks
- 3 tablespoons olive oil Pinch salt
- 1/8 teaspoon cayenne pepper
- 1 teaspoon paprika
- 2 tablespoons lemon juice

Directions:

1. Prepare and preheat grill. Slice fennel bulbs lengthwise into ½" slices, leaving the stalks and fronds attached.
2. Brush fennel and haddock with olive oil on all sides to coat. Sprinkle fish with salt, pepper, and paprika. Place fennel on grill 6″ above medium coals, cut side down. Arrange fish on top of fennel and close the grill.
3. Grill for 5–7 minutes or until fennel is deep golden brown and fish flakes when tested with fork. Remove fish to serving platter, sprinkle with lemon juice, and cover.
4. Cut the root end and stems from the fennel and discard. Slice fennel and place on top of fish; serve immediately.

Nutrition Info:

- Info Per Serving: Calories: 246.68; Fat: 11.35 g ;Saturated fat:1.58 g ;Sodium: 192.31 mg

Citrus Cod Bake

Servings: 2
Cooking Time: 25 Min
Ingredients:

- 2 tbsp. garlic, crushed
- 1 tbsp. olive oil
- 2 rosemary sprigs, stem removed and finely chopped
- 2 oregano sprigs, finely chopped
- 2 cod fillets, rinsed and patted dry
- ¼ tsp Himalayan pink salt
- ¼ tsp ground black pepper
- 1 lime, cut into 4 round slices
- ½ lemon, wedged

Directions:

1. Heat the oven to 450°F gas mark 8.
2. In a small-sized mixing bowl, add the garlic, olive oil, rosemary, and oregano, mix to combine.
3. Place the cod fillets on a baking sheet and season with salt and pepper.
4. Evenly coat both cod fillets with the garlic and herb mixture. Place 2 lime slices on each fillet. Bake for 18 to 25 minutes, or until the cod fillets are completely cooked.
5. Serve with a lemon wedge.

Nutrition Info:

- Info Per Serving: Calories: 218 ; Fat:3 g ;Saturated fat: 1 g ;Sodium: 430 mg

Shrimp Stir-fry

Servings: 2
Cooking Time: 15 Min
Ingredients:

- 12 oz zucchini spirals
- 2 tsp low-sodium tamari sauce
- 2 tsp apple cider vinegar
- 1 tsp ginger, peeled and grated
- 1 tsp garlic, crushed
- 1 tsp organic honey
- 2 tsp sesame oil
- 6 oz shrimp, peeled and deveined
- 2 cups napa cabbage, shredded
- 1 medium green bell pepper, thinly sliced
- 1 spring onion, thinly sliced
- 1 tbsp. toasted sesame seeds, for garnish

Directions:

1. Cook the zucchini according to the package directions. Drain and run under cold water to stop the cooking process. Transfer the zucchini to a medium-sized mixing bowl and set aside.
2. In a small-sized mixing bowl, add the tamari sauce, apple cider vinegar, ginger, garlic, and honey, mix to combine, and set aside.
3. Warm the sesame oil in a medium-sized, heavy-bottom pan over medium-high heat. Add the shrimp and fry for 5 minutes until cooked through.
4. Add the napa cabbage, green bell pepper, and spring onion and fry for 4 minutes until the vegetables are tender. Add the tamari sauce mixture and the zucchini, toss to coat, heat for 1 minute.
5. Serve into bowls and top with sesame seeds.

Nutrition Info:

- Info Per Serving: Calories: 400 ; Fat: 8 g ;Saturated fat: 1 g ;Sodium: 347 mg

Tuna Patties

Servings: 6
Cooking Time: 10 Min
Ingredients:

- 12 oz canned, water-packed tuna, drained
- 4 tbsp. almond flour
- 1 large free-range egg white
- 1 tbsp. brown onion, finely chopped
- ½ lemon, juiced
- ½ tsp parsley, finely chopped

- Pinch red pepper flakes
- Pinch Himalayan pink salt
- Pinch ground black pepper
- Cooking spray

Directions:

1. In a medium-sized mixing bowl, add the tuna, almond flour, egg white, onions, lemon juice, parsley, red pepper flakes, salt, and pepper, mix to combine.

2. Mold the tuna mixture into 6 equal patties.

3. Place the tuna cakes on a plate and chill for 1 hour in the refrigerator until firm.

4. Spray a large, heavy-bottom pan with cooking spray and place it over medium-high heat.

5. Add the tuna cakes to the pan and cook for 5 minutes per side, turning once, until browned and heated through. Serve.

Nutrition Info:

- Info Per Serving: Calories: 243 ; Fat: 6 g ;Saturated fat: 0 g ;Sodium: 558 mg

Baked Halibut In Mustard Sauce

Servings: 4

Cooking Time: X

Ingredients:

- 1 pound halibut fillet Pinch of salt
- 1/8 teaspoon white pepper
- 1 tablespoon lemon juice
- 1 teaspoon orange zest
- 2 tablespoons butter or margarine, melted
- ¼ cup skim milk
- 2 tablespoons Dijon mustard
- 1 slice Honey-Wheat Sesame Bread , crumbled

Directions:

1. Preheat oven to 400ºF. Spray a 1-quart baking dish with nonstick cooking spray. Cut fish into serving-size pieces and sprinkle with salt, pepper, and lemon juice.

2. In small bowl, combine melted butter, milk, and mustard, and whisk until blended. Stir in the breadcrumbs. Pour this sauce over the fish.

3. Bake for 20–25 minutes, or until fish flakes when tested with fork and sauce is bubbling. Serve immediately.

Nutrition Info:

- Info Per Serving: Calories: 219.84 ; Fat:9.38 g ;Saturated fat: 4.30 g ;Sodium: 244.95 mg

Scallops On Skewers With Tomatoes

Servings: 4

Cooking Time: X

Ingredients:

- 1 pound sea scallops
- 12 cherry tomatoes
- 4 green onions, cut in half crosswise
- ½ cup chopped parsley

- 1 tablespoon fresh oregano leaves
- 3 tablespoons olive oil
- 2 tablespoons lemon juice
- 2 cloves garlic
- 1/8 teaspoon salt
- 1/8 teaspoon pepper

Directions:

1. Prepare and preheat broiler. Rinse scallops and pat dry. Thread on skewers along with cherry tomatoes and green onions.

2. In blender or food processor, combine remaining ingredients. Blend or process until smooth. Reserve ¼ cup of this sauce.

3. Brush remaining sauce onto the food on the skewers. Place on broiler pan. Broil 6″ from heat for 3–4 minutes per side, turning once during cooking time. Serve with remaining sauce.

Nutrition Info:

- Info Per Serving: Calories:202.03 ; Fat:11.11 g ;Saturated fat: 1.52 g ;Sodium:251.50 mg

Spicy Catfish Tacos

Servings: 2

Cooking Time: 15 Min

Ingredients:

- 1 cup red cabbage, shredded
- 1 medium carrot, peeled and shredded
- ½ spring onion, finely chopped
- ¼ cup fat-free sour cream
- 2 tsp hot sauce, (optional)
- 1 tsp lime juice
- 2 (5 oz) catfish fillets
- ¼ tsp ground cumin
- Himalayan pink salt
- Ground black pepper
- Cooking spray
- 4 whole-grain tortillas

Directions:

1. In a medium-sized mixing bowl, add the cabbage, carrots, spring onion, sour cream, hot sauce (if using), and lime juice, mix until combined. Set aside.

2. Season both sides of the catfish with cumin, salt, and pepper.

3. Spray a medium-sized, heavy-bottom pan with cooking spray and place it over medium-high heat. Add the catfish fillets and cook for 6 minutes per side, turning once, until cooked completely through.

4. Divide the catfish among the tortillas and top with the spicy cabbage slaw. Serve.

Nutrition Info:

- Info Per Serving: Calories: 305 ; Fat: 3 g ;Saturated fat: 0 g ;Sodium: 295 mg

Red Snapper With Fruit Salsa

Servings: 4
Cooking Time: X
Ingredients:

- 1 cup blueberries
- 1 cup chopped watermelon
- 1 jalapeño pepper, minced
- ½ cup chopped tomatoes
- 3 tablespoons olive oil, divided
- 2 tablespoons orange juice
- 1/8 teaspoon salt, divided
- 1/8 teaspoon white pepper
- 4 (4-ounce) red snapper fillets
- 1 lemon, thinly sliced

Directions:

1. Preheat oven to 400ºF. Spray a 9″ glass baking pan with nonstick cooking spray and set aside. In medium bowl, combine blueberries, watermelon, jalapeño pepper, tomatoes, 1 tablespoon olive oil, orange juice, and half of the salt. Mix well and set aside.

2. Arrange fillets in prepared pan. Sprinkle with remaining salt and the white pepper and drizzle with 2 tablespoons olive oil. Top with lemon slices.

3. Bake for 15 to 20 minutes, or until fish is opaque and flesh flakes when tested with fork. Place on serving plate and top with blueberry mixture; serve immediately.

Nutrition Info:

- Info Per Serving: Calories: 254.40; Fat:12.01 g ;Saturated fat:1.82 g ;Sodium:186.42 mg

Poached Fish With Tomatoes And Capers

Servings: 4
Cooking Time: X
Ingredients:

- 2 tablespoons olive oil
- ½ cup chopped red onion
- 2 cloves garlic, minced
- 1 cup chopped fresh tomatoes
- 2 tablespoons no-salt tomato paste
- ¼ cup dry white wine
- 2 tablespoons capers, rinsed
- 4 (4-ounce) white fish fillets
- ¼ cup chopped parsley

Directions:

1. In large skillet, heat olive oil over medium heat. Add onion and garlic; cook and stir until tender, about 5 minutes. Add tomatoes, tomato paste, and wine and bring to a simmer; simmer for 5 minutes, stirring frequently.

2. Add capers to sauce and stir, then arrange fillets on top of sauce. Spoon sauce over fish. Reduce heat to low, cover, and poach for 7–10 minutes, or until fish flakes when tested with fork. Sprinkle with parsley and serve immediately.

Nutrition Info:

- Info Per Serving: Calories: 191.05 ; Fat:7.70 g ;Saturated fat: 1.13 g ;Sodium: 199.73 mg

Seafood Risotto

Servings: 6
Cooking Time: X
Ingredients:

- 2 cups water
- 2½ cups Low-Sodium Chicken Broth
- 2 tablespoons olive oil
- 1 onion, minced
- 3 cloves garlic, minced
- 1½ cups Arborio rice
- 1 cup chopped celery
- 1 tablespoon fresh dill weed
- ¼ cup dry white wine
- ½ pound sole fillets
- ¼ pound small raw shrimp
- ½ pound bay scallops
- ¼ cup grated Parmesan cheese
- 1 tablespoon butter

Directions:

1. In medium saucepan, combine water and broth and heat over low heat. Keep mixture on heat.

2. In large saucepan, heat olive oil over medium heat. Add onion and garlic; cook and stir until crisp-tender, about 3 minutes. Add rice; cook and stir for 3 minutes.

3. Start adding broth mixture, a cup at a time, stirring frequently, adding liquid when previous addition is absorbed. When only 1 cup of broth remains to be added, stir in celery, dill, wine, fish fillets, shrimp, and scallops to rice mixture. Add last cup of broth.

4. Cook, stirring constantly, for 5–7 minutes or until fish is cooked and rice is tender and creamy. Stir in Parmesan and butter, stir, and serve.

Nutrition Info:

- Info Per Serving: Calories:397.22 ; Fat:11.11 g ;Saturated fat:3.20 g ;Sodium:354.58 mg

Bluefish With Asian Seasonings

Servings: 4
Cooking Time: X
Ingredients:

- 1¼ pounds bluefish fillets
- 1 tablespoon lime juice
- 2 teaspoons low-sodium soy sauce
- 2 teaspoons grated ginger root
- 3 cloves garlic, minced
- 1 teaspoon sesame oil
- 1 teaspoon Thai chile paste

- 1 tablespoon orange juice
- 1/8 teaspoon white pepper

Directions:

1. Preheat broiler. Place bluefish fillets on a broiler pan. In small bowl, combine all remaining ingredients, being very careful to make sure that the chile paste is evenly distributed in the sauce.

2. Pour sauce over the fillets. Broil 6″ from heat for 6–9 minutes or until fish is opaque and flakes when tested with fork. Serve immediately.

Nutrition Info:

- Info Per Serving: Calories: 193.98 ; Fat:7.17 g ;Saturated fat: 1.46 g ;Sodium: 181.39 mg

Sesame-crusted Mahi Mahi

Servings: 4
Cooking Time: X

Ingredients:

- 4 (4-ounce) mahi mahi or sole fillets
- 2 tablespoons Dijon mustard
- 1 tablespoon low-fat sour cream
- ½ cup sesame seeds
- 2 tablespoons olive oil
- 1 lemon, cut into wedges

Directions:

1. Rinse fillets and pat dry. In small bowl, combine mustard and sour cream and mix well. Spread this mixture on all sides of fish. Roll in sesame seeds to coat.

2. Heat olive oil in large skillet over medium heat. Pan-fry fish, turning once, for 5–8 minutes or until fish flakes when tested with fork and sesame seeds are toasted. Serve immediately with lemon wedges.

Nutrition Info:

- Info Per Serving: Calories: 282.75; Fat: 17.17 g ;Saturated fat:2.84 g ;Sodium: 209.54 mg

Halibut Burgers

Servings: 4
Cooking Time: 35 Min

Ingredients:

- Aluminum foil
- 1 lb. halibut fillets
- ½ tsp Himalayan pink salt, divided
- ¼ tsp ground black pepper
- ½ cup whole wheat breadcrumbs
- 1 large free-range egg
- 1 tbsp. garlic, crushed
- ½ tsp dried dill
- 2 tbsp. avocado oil
- 4 whole wheat buns

Directions:

1. Heat the oven to 400°F gas mark 6. Line a baking sheet with aluminum foil.

2. Place the halibut fillets on the baking sheet and season with ¼ tsp salt and pepper. Bake for 15 to 20 minutes, or until the halibut flakes with a fork. Remove from the oven.

3. Transfer the flesh into a medium-sized mixing bowl, removing any bones.

4. Add the breadcrumbs, egg, garlic, dill and the remaining ¼ tsp salt, mix to combine.

5. Mold the fish mixture into 4 patties.

6. Heat the avocado oil in a large heavy bottom pan over medium heat.

7. Gently place the halibut patties in the pan. Fry for 5 to 6 minutes, until browned, flip, and cook for 3 to 5 minutes, remove from the heat.

8. Place 1 fish patty on each of the 4 buns and serve.

Nutrition Info:

- Info Per Serving: Calories: 294 ; Fat: 16 g ;Saturated fat: 3 g ;Sodium: 458 mg

Scallops On Skewers With Lemon

Servings: 4
Cooking Time: X

Ingredients:

- 2 tablespoons lemon juice
- 1 teaspoon grated lemon zest
- 2 teaspoons sesame oil
- 2 tablespoons chili sauce
- 1/8 teaspoon cayenne pepper
- 1 pound sea scallops
- 4 strips low-sodium bacon

Directions:

1. Prepare and preheat grill or broiler. In medium bowl, combine lemon juice, zest, sesame oil, chili sauce, and cayenne pepper and mix well. Add scallops and toss to coat. Let stand for 15 minutes.

2. Make skewers with the scallops and bacon. Thread a skewer through one end of the bacon, then add a scallop. Curve the bacon around the scallop and thread onto the skewer so it surrounds the scallop halfway. Repeat with 3 to 4 more scallops and the bacon slice.

3. Repeat with remaining scallops and bacon. Grill or broil 6″ from heat source for 3–5 minutes per side, until bacon is crisp and scallops are cooked and opaque. Serve immediately.

Nutrition Info:

- Info Per Serving: Calories:173.65 ; Fat:6.48 g ;Saturated fat: 1.51 g;Sodium:266.64 mg

Broiled Swordfish

Servings: 4
Cooking Time: X
Ingredients:
- 1 tablespoon olive oil
- 2 tablespoons dry white wine
- 1 teaspoon lemon zest
- ¼ teaspoon salt
- 1/8 teaspoon white pepper
- 1 teaspoon dried dill weed
- 1¼ pounds swordfish steaks
- 4 ½-inch-thick tomato slices

Directions:
1. Preheat broiler. In small bowl, combine oil, wine, zest, salt, pepper, and dill weed and whisk to blend.
2. Place steaks on broiler pan. Brush steaks with oil mixture. Broil 6″ from heat for 4 minutes. Turn fish and brush with remaining oil mixture. Top with tomatoes. Return to broiler and broil for 4–6 minutes or until fish flakes when tested with fork.

Nutrition Info:
- Info Per Serving: Calories: 210.97 ; Fat:9.10 g ;Saturated fat: 2.03 g ;Sodium:273.91 mg

Sesame-pepper Salmon Kabobs

Servings: 4
Cooking Time: X
Ingredients:
- 1 pound salmon steak
- 2 tablespoons olive oil, divided
- ¼ cup sesame seeds
- 1 teaspoon pepper
- 1 red bell pepper
- 1 yellow bell pepper
- 1 red onion
- 8 cremini mushrooms
- 1/8 teaspoon salt

Directions:
1. Prepare and preheat grill. Cut salmon steak into 1″ pieces, discarding skin and bones. Brush salmon with half of the olive oil.
2. In small bowl, combine sesame seeds and pepper and mix. Press all sides of salmon cubes into the sesame seed mixture.
3. Slice bell peppers into 1″ slices and cut red onion into 8 wedges; trim mushroom stems and leave caps whole. Skewer coated salmon pieces, peppers, onion, and mushrooms on metal skewers. Brush vegetables with remaining olive oil and sprinkle with salt.
4. Grill 6″ from medium coals, turning once during cooking time, until the sesame seeds are very brown and toasted and fish is just done, about 6–8 minutes. Serve immediately.

Nutrition Info:
- Info Per Serving: Calories:319.33 ; Fat:20.26 g ;Saturated fat: 3.67 g ;Sodium:141.88 mg

Baked Lemon Sole With Herbed Crumbs

Servings: 4
Cooking Time: X
Ingredients:
- 2 slices Light Whole-Grain Bread , crumbled
- 2 tablespoons minced parsley
- 2 cloves garlic, minced
- 1 teaspoon dried dill weed
- 2 tablespoons olive oil
- 4 (6-ounce) sole fillets
- 2 tablespoons lemon juice Pinch salt
- 1/8 teaspoon white pepper

Directions:
1. Preheat oven to 350ºF. In small bowl, combine breadcrumbs, parsley, garlic, and dill weed, and mix well. Drizzle with olive oil and toss to coat.
2. Spray a 9″ baking dish with nonstick cooking spray and arrange fillets in dish. Sprinkle with lemon juice, salt, and pepper. Divide crumb mixture on top of fillets.
3. Bake for 12–17 minutes or until fish flakes when tested with a fork and crumb topping is browned. Serve immediately.

Nutrition Info:
- Info Per Serving: Calories: 294.58; Fat:9.86 g ;Saturated fat:1.65 g ;Sodium:288.21 mg

Salmon With Mustard And Orange

Servings: 4
Cooking Time: X
Ingredients:
- 4 (5-ounce) salmon fillets
- 1 tablespoon olive oil
- 2 tablespoons Dijon mustard
- 1 tablespoon flour
- 1 teaspoon orange zest
- 2 tablespoons orange juice Pinch salt
- 1/8 teaspoon white pepper

Directions:
1. Preheat broiler. Place fillets on a broiler pan. In small bowl, combine remaining ingredients and mix well. Spread over salmon.
2. Broil fish 6″ from heat for 7–10 minutes or until fish flakes when tested with fork and topping bubbles and begins to brown. Serve immediately.

Nutrition Info:
- Info Per Serving: Calories: 277.64; Fat:14.02 g ;Saturated fat:2.09 g ;Sodium:197.84 mg

Seared Scallops With Fruit

Servings: 3–4
Cooking Time: X
Ingredients:

- 1 pound sea scallops Pinch salt
- 1/8 teaspoon white pepper
- 1 tablespoon olive oil
- 1 tablespoon butter or margarine
- ¼ cup dry white wine
- 2 peaches, sliced
- 1 cup blueberries
- 1 tablespoon lime juice

Directions:

1. Rinse scallops and pat dry. Sprinkle with salt and pepper and set aside.
2. In large skillet, heat olive oil and butter over medium-high heat. Add the scallops and don't move them for 3 minutes. Carefully check to see if the scallops are deep golden brown. If they are, turn and cook for 1–2 minutes on the second side.
3. Remove scallops to serving plate. Add peaches to skillet and brown quickly on one side, about 2 minutes. Turn peaches and add wine to skillet; bring to a boil. Remove from heat and add blueberries. Pour over scallops, sprinkle with lime juice, and serve immediately.

Nutrition Info:

- Info Per Serving: Calories: 207.89; Fat: 7.36 g ;Saturated fat:2.40 g ;Sodium: 242.16 mg

Crispy Mixed Nut Fish Fillets

Servings: 4
Cooking Time: 15 Minutes
Ingredients:

- 4 (6-ounce) white fish fillets, such as red snapper or cod
- 2 tablespoons low-sodium yellow mustard
- 2 tablespoons nonfat plain Greek yogurt
- 2 tablespoons low-fat buttermilk
- 1 teaspoon dried Italian herb seasoning
- ⅛ teaspoon white pepper
- ¼ cup hazelnut flour
- 2 tablespoons almond flour
- 2 tablespoons ground almonds
- 2 tablespoons ground hazelnuts

Directions:

1. Preheat the oven to 400°F. Line a baking sheet with a fine wire rack and set aside.
2. Pat the fish dry and place on a plate.
3. In a shallow bowl, combine the mustard, yogurt, buttermilk, Italian seasoning, and white pepper.
4. On a plate, combine the hazelnut flour and almond flour, and add the ground almonds, the ground hazelnuts, and mix well.

5. Coat the fish with the mustard mixture, then coat with the nut mixture. Place on the prepared baking sheet.
6. Bake the fish for 12 to 17 minutes, until it flakes when tested with a fork. Serve immediately.

Nutrition Info:

- Info Per Serving: Calories: 256 ; Fat: 9 g ;Saturated fat: 1 g;Sodium: 206 mg

Shrimp And Pineapple Lettuce Wraps

Servings: 4
Cooking Time: 12 Minutes
Ingredients:

- 2 teaspoons olive oil
- 2 jalapeño peppers, seeded and minced
- 6 scallions, chopped
- 2 yellow bell peppers, seeded and chopped
- 8 ounces small shrimp, peeled and deveined
- 2 cups canned pineapple chunks, drained, reserving juice
- 2 tablespoons fresh lime juice
- 1 avocado, peeled, and cubed
- 1 large carrot, coarsely grated
- 8 romaine or Boston lettuce leaves, rinsed and dried

Directions:

1. In a medium saucepan, heat the olive oil over medium heat.
2. Add the jalapeño pepper and scallions and cook for 2 minutes, stirring constantly.
3. Add the bell pepper, and cook for 2 minutes.
4. Add the shrimp, and cook for 1 minute, stirring constantly.
5. Add the pineapple, 2 tablespoons of the reserved pineapple juice, and lime juice, and bring to a simmer. Simmer for 1 minute longer or until the shrimp curl and turn pink. Let the mixture cool for 5 minutes.
6. Serve the shrimp mixture with the cubed avocado and grated carrot, wrapped in the lettuce leaves.

Nutrition Info:

- Info Per Serving: Calories: 241 ; Fat: 9 g ;Saturated fat: 2 g;Sodium: 109 mg

Sole Medallions Poached In Wine

Servings: 3
Cooking Time: X
Ingredients:

- 1 pound sole fillet Pinch salt
- 1/8 teaspoon white pepper
- ½ cup Low-Sodium Chicken Broth
- ½ cup dry white wine
- 2 shallots, minced
- ½ cup low-fat, low-sodium mayonnaise
- ½ teaspoon dried thyme leaves

- 2 tablespoons lemon juice
- ½ cup blueberries

Directions:

1. Cut sole fillet into 1″ wide strips. Roll up strips; secure with toothpicks. Sprinkle fish with salt and pepper.
2. In saucepan just large enough to hold the fish, combine chicken broth, wine, and shallots. Bring to a simmer, then lower heat to low. Add fish, cover, and poach for 10–15 minutes or until fish is just opaque. Remove from poaching liquid and remove toothpicks.
3. In small bowl, combine mayonnaise, thyme, lemon juice, and blueberries, and stir to blend. Serve with fish.

Nutrition Info:

- Info Per Serving: Calories: 240.38; Fat:8.93 g ;Saturated fat: 1.64 g ;Sodium: 207.97 mg

Cod And Potatoes

Servings: 4
Cooking Time: X
Ingredients:

- 3 Yukon Gold potatoes
- ¼ cup olive oil
- 1/8 teaspoon white pepper
- 1½ teaspoons dried herbs de Provence, divided
- 4 (4-ounce) cod steaks
- 1 tablespoon butter or margarine
- 2 tablespoons lemon juice

Directions:

1. Preheat oven to 350ºF. Spray a 9″ glass baking dish with nonstick cooking spray. Thinly slice the potatoes. Layer in the baking dish, drizzling each layer with a tablespoon of olive oil, a sprinkle of pepper, and some of the herbs de Provence.
2. Bake for 35–45 minutes or until potatoes are browned on top and tender when pierced with a fork. Arrange cod steaks on top of potatoes. Dot with butter and sprinkle with lemon juice and remaining herbs de Provence.
3. Bake for 15–25 minutes longer or until fish flakes when tested with fork.

Nutrition Info:

- Info Per Serving: Calories: 362.62 ; Fat:17.28 g ;Saturated fat: 3.88 g ;Sodium: 91.56 mg

Flounder Fillet Bake

Servings: 4
Cooking Time: 15 Min
Ingredients:

- Aluminum foil
- 4 (4 oz) flounder fillets
- 2 tbsp. avocado oil
- 1 tsp ground thyme
- ½ tsp Himalayan pink salt
- ¼ tsp ground black pepper

- 1 lime, cut into wedges
- 2 tbsp. cilantro, finely chopped

Directions:

1. Heat the oven to 400°F gas mark 6. Line a baking sheet with aluminum foil.
2. Place the flounder fillets on the baking sheet and drizzle with avocado oil.
3. Season both sides of the fillets with thyme, salt pepper.
4. Bake for 6 to 8 minutes, flip, and bake for a further 5 minutes, or until cooked through. Remove from the oven.
5. Serve the flounder fillets with a lime wedge and sprinkle with cilantro.

Nutrition Info:

- Info Per Serving: Calories: 164 ; Fat: 8 g ;Saturated fat: 1 g ;Sodium: 369 mg

Salmon With Farro Pilaf

Servings: 4
Cooking Time: 25 Minutes
Ingredients:

- ½ cup farro
- 1¼ cups low-sodium vegetable broth
- 4 (4-ounce) salmon fillets
- Pinch salt
- ½ teaspoon dried marjoram leaves
- ⅛ teaspoon white pepper
- ¼ cup dried cherries
- ¼ cup dried currants
- 1 cup fresh baby spinach leaves
- 1 tablespoon orange juice

Directions:

1. Preheat the oven to 400°F. Line a baking sheet with parchment paper and set aside.
2. In a medium saucepan over medium heat, combine the farro and the vegetable broth and bring to a simmer. Reduce the heat to low and simmer, partially covered, for 25 minutes, or until the farro is tender.
3. Meanwhile, sprinkle the salmon with the salt, marjoram, and white pepper and place on the prepared baking sheet.
4. When the farro has cooked for 10 minutes, bake the salmon in the oven for 12 to 15 minutes, or until the salmon flakes when tested with a fork. Remove and cover to keep warm.
5. When the farro is tender, add the cherries, currants, spinach, and orange juice; stir and cover. Let stand off the heat for 2 to 3 minutes.
6. Plate the salmon and serve with the farro pilaf.

Nutrition Info:

- Info Per Serving: Calories: 304 ; Fat: 8 g ;Saturated fat: 2 g;Sodium: 139 mg

Vietnamese Fish And Noodle Bowl

Servings: 3
Cooking Time: 15 Minutes
Ingredients:

- ¾ pound grouper fillets, cut into 1-inch pieces
- 1 tablespoon cornstarch
- ⅛ teaspoon cayenne pepper
- 2 teaspoons fish sauce
- 1 tablespoon rice wine vinegar
- 1 teaspoon sugar
- 2 tablespoons fresh lemon juice
- 1 teaspoon olive oil
- ¼ cup minced daikon radish
- 3 cloves garlic, minced
- 4 ounces whole-wheat spaghetti, broken in half
- 1½ cups low-sodium vegetable broth
- 2 tablespoons chopped peanuts
- 2 tablespoons minced fresh cilantro
- 2 tablespoons minced fresh basil

Directions:

1. In a medium bowl, toss the grouper with the cornstarch and cayenne pepper and set aside.
2. In a small bowl, combine the fish sauce, rice wine vinegar, sugar, and lemon juice, and stir to mix well.
3. In a large skillet, heat the olive oil over medium heat. Add the daikon and garlic and cook for 1 minute, stirring constantly.
4. Add the fish to the skillet; sauté for 2 to 3 minutes, stirring frequently, until the fish browns lightly.
5. Remove the fish mixture to a large bowl and set aside.
6. Add the spaghetti and vegetable broth to the skillet, and stir. Bring to a simmer over high heat and cook for 7 to 8 minutes or until the pasta is al dente.
7. Return the fish and radish mixture to the skillet along with the fish sauce mixture, peanuts, cilantro, and basil. Toss for 1 minute, then serve immediately in bowls.

Nutrition Info:

- Info Per Serving: Calories: 324 ; Fat: 6 g ;Saturated fat: 1 g;Sodium: 439 mg

Pistachio-crusted Red Snapper

Servings: 4
Cooking Time: X
Ingredients:

- 1 tablespoon lemon juice
- 1 teaspoon grated orange zest
- 1 teaspoon grated lemon zest
- 2 tablespoons olive oil
- 1/3 cup chopped pistachios
- 1 slice Light Whole-Grain Bread , crumbled
- 1 pound red snapper fillets Pinch salt
- 1/8 teaspoon pepper

Directions:

1. Preheat oven to 375ºF. In small bowl, combine lemon juice, orange zest, lemon zest, and olive oil. In another small bowl, combine chopped pistachios and crumbled bread. Drizzle lemon mixture over bread mixture and toss to coat.
2. Spray a 9″-square glass baking dish with nonstick cooking spray. Arrange fish in dish and sprinkle with salt and pepper. Top evenly with the crumb mixture, patting into place.
3. Bake for 15–25 minutes, or until fish is opaque and flakes when tested with fork and crumb mixture is browned. Serve immediately.

Nutrition Info:

- Info Per Serving: Calories: 283.52; Fat: 15.79 g ;Saturated fat:2.20 g ;Sodium: 172.06 mg

Healthy Paella

Servings: 4
Cooking Time: 15 Minutes
Ingredients:

- 1 tablespoon olive oil
- 1 onion, chopped
- 3 cloves garlic, minced
- 1 red bell pepper, seeded and chopped
- 2½ cups low-sodium vegetable broth
- 1 tomato, chopped
- 1 teaspoon smoked paprika
- 1 teaspoon dried thyme leaves
- ¼ teaspoon turmeric
- ⅛ teaspoon black pepper
- 1 cup whole-wheat orzo
- ½ pound halibut fillets, cut into 1-inch pieces
- 12 medium shrimp, peeled and deveined
- ¼ cup chopped fresh flat-leaf parsley

Directions:

1. In a large deep skillet, heat the olive oil over medium heat.
2. Add the onion, garlic, and red bell pepper, and cook, stirring, for 2 minutes.
3. Add the vegetable broth, tomato, paprika, thyme, turmeric, and black pepper, and bring to a simmer.
4. Stir in the orzo, making sure it is submerged in the liquid in the pan. Simmer for 5 minutes, stirring occasionally.
5. Add the halibut and stir. Simmer for 4 minutes.
6. Add the shrimp and stir. Simmer for 2 to 3 minutes or until the shrimp curl and turn pink and the pasta is cooked al dente.
7. Sprinkle with the parsley, and serve immediately.

Nutrition Info:

- Info Per Serving: Calories: 367 ; Fat: 7 g ;Saturated fat: 1 g;Sodium: 147 mg

Cod Satay

Servings: 4
Cooking Time: 15 Minutes
Ingredients:

- 2 teaspoons olive oil, divided
- 1 small onion, diced
- 2 cloves garlic, minced
- ⅓ cup low-fat coconut milk
- 1 tomato, chopped
- 2 tablespoons low-fat peanut butter
- 1 tablespoon packed brown sugar
- ⅓ cup low-sodium vegetable broth
- 2 teaspoons low-sodium soy sauce
- ⅛ teaspoon ground ginger
- Pinch red pepper flakes
- 4 (6-ounce) cod fillets
- ⅛ teaspoon white pepper

Directions:

1. In a small saucepan, heat 1 teaspoon of the olive oil over medium heat.
2. Add the onion and garlic, and cook, stirring frequently for 3 minutes.
3. Add the coconut milk, tomato, peanut butter, brown sugar, broth, soy sauce, ginger, and red pepper flakes, and bring to a simmer, stirring with a whisk until the sauce combines. Simmer for 2 minutes, then remove the satay sauce from the heat and set aside.
4. Season the cod with the white pepper.
5. Heat a large nonstick skillet with the remaining 1 teaspoon olive oil, and add the cod fillets. Cook for 3 minutes, then turn and cook for 3 to 4 minutes more or until the fish flakes when tested with a fork.
6. Cover the fish with the satay sauce and serve immediately.

Nutrition Info:

- Info Per Serving: Calories: 255 ; Fat: 10 g ;Saturated fat: 5 g;Sodium: 222 mg

Salmon Vegetable Stir-fry

Servings: 4
Cooking Time: X
Ingredients:

- 2 tablespoons rice vinegar
- 1 tablespoon sugar
- 1 tablespoon grated ginger root
- 1 tablespoon cornstarch
- 2 tablespoons hoisin sauce
- 1/8 teaspoon white pepper
- 2 tablespoons peanut oil
- 1 onion, sliced
- ½ pound sugar-snap peas
- 3 carrots, sliced
- 1 red bell pepper, sliced
- ¼ pound salmon fillet

Directions:

1. In small bowl, combine rice vinegar, sugar, ginger root, cornstarch, hoi-sin sauce, and pepper. Mix well and set aside.
2. In large skillet or wok, heat peanut oil over high heat. Add onion, peas, and carrots. Stir-fry for 3–4 minutes or until vegetables begin to soften. Add red bell pepper.
3. Immediately place salmon fillet on top of vegetables. Reduce heat to medium, cover skillet or wok and cook for 4–5 minutes or until salmon flakes when tested with fork.
4. Stir the vinegar mixture and add to skillet or wok. Turn heat to medium-high and stir-fry to break up the salmon for 2–3 minutes until the sauce bubbles and thickens. Serve immediately over hot cooked rice.

Nutrition Info:

- Info Per Serving: Calories: 371.71; Fat:11.73 g ;Saturated fat: 3.24 g ;Sodium: 237.60 mg

Vegetarian Mains

Farro Sloppy Joes

Servings: X
Cooking Time: 20 Minutes
Ingredients:

- ¾ cup uncooked pearled farro, rinsed well
- 1 cup water
- 1 teaspoon olive oil
- 1 red bell pepper, chopped
- ½ cup sweet onion, finely chopped
- 1 teaspoon minced garlic
- 1 (15-ounce) can low-sodium diced tomatoes, with their juices
- 1 teaspoon maple syrup
- 1 teaspoon low-sodium tamari sauce
- ½ teaspoon chili powder
- ¼ teaspoon dry mustard
- ¼ teaspoon dried oregano
- 2 whole-grain hamburger rolls, for serving

Directions:

1. In a small saucepan, combine the farro with the water. Bring to a boil over high heat and then reduce the heat to low. Cover and simmer until the water is absorbed, 15 to 20 minutes. Drain any excess water.
2. While the farro is cooking, warm the oil in a medium skillet and sauté the bell pepper, onions, and garlic until softened, about 3 minutes.
3. Stir in the tomatoes, maple syrup, tamari, chili powder, mustard, and oregano and bring the sauce to a boil. Reduce the heat to low and simmer for 5 to 7 minutes, stirring occasionally.
4. Remove the sauce from the heat and stir in the cooked farro.
5. Divide the sloppy joe mixture between the rolls and serve.

Nutrition Info:

- Info Per Serving: Calories: 407 ; Fat: 6 g ;Saturated fat: 1 g ;Sodium: 282 mg

Rice-and-vegetable Casserole

Servings: 8
Cooking Time: X
Ingredients:

- 1 tablespoon olive oil
- 2 onions, chopped
- 1 (8-ounce) package sliced mushrooms
- 2 red bell peppers, chopped
- 1 jalapeño pepper, minced
- 4 cups cooked brown rice
- 1½ cups milk
- 1 egg
- 2 egg whites
- ½ cup low-fat sour cream
- 1 cup shredded part-skim mozzarella cheese
- ½ cup shredded Colby cheese

Directions:

1. Preheat oven to 350ºF. Spray a 13″ × 9″ baking pan with nonstick cooking spray and set aside.
2. In large saucepan, heat olive oil. Add onions and mushrooms; cook and stir for 3 minutes. Then add bell peppers and jalapeño pepper; cook and stir for 3–4 minutes longer until vegetables are crisp-tender.
3. In large bowl, combine rice, milk, egg, egg whites, sour cream, mozzarella cheese, and Colby cheese. Layer half of this mixture in the prepared baking pan. Top with vegetables, then top with remaining rice mixture. Bake for 50–65 minutes or until casserole is bubbling, set, and beginning to brown. Let stand for 5 minutes, then cut into squares to serve.

Nutrition Info:

- Info Per Serving: Calories:276.42; Fat:10.87 g ;Saturated fat:5.35 g ;Sodium: 175.20 mg

Corn-and-chili Pancakes

Servings: 6
Cooking Time: X
Ingredients:

- ½ cup buttermilk
- 1 tablespoon olive oil
- ½ cup egg substitute
- ½ cup grated extra-sharp Cheddar cheese
- 1 jalapeño pepper, minced
- 2 ears sweet corn
- ½ cup cornmeal
- 1 cup all-purpose flour
- 1½ teaspoons baking powder
- ½ teaspoon baking soda
- 1 tablespoon sugar
- 1 tablespoon chili powder
- 1 tablespoon peanut oil
- 1 tablespoon butter

Directions:

1. In large bowl, combine buttermilk, olive oil, egg substitute, Cheddar, and jalapeño pepper and mix well.
2. Cut the kernels off the sweet corn and add to buttermilk mixture along with cornmeal, flour, baking powder, baking soda, sugar, and chili powder; mix until combined. Let stand for 10 minutes.
3. Heat griddle or frying pan over medium heat. Brush with the butter, then add the batter, ¼ cup at a time. Cook

until bubbles form and start to break and sides look dry, about 3–4 minutes. Carefully flip pancakes and cook until light golden brown on second side, about 2–3 minutes. Serve immediately.

Nutrition Info:
- Info Per Serving: Calories:252.62; Fat: 9.20 g ;Saturated fat:3.03 g ;Sodium:287.01 mg

Florentine Quinoa Casserole

Servings: X
Cooking Time: 25 Minutes
Ingredients:
- Nonstick olive oil cooking spray
- 2 teaspoons olive oil
- 1 carrot, shredded
- ½ sweet onion, chopped
- 1 cup sliced mushrooms
- 1 teaspoon minced garlic
- 1 tablespoon whole-wheat flour
- 1 cup unsweetened soy milk
- ⅛ teaspoon ground nutmeg
- Sea salt
- Freshly ground black pepper
- 2 cups cooked quinoa
- 1 cup packed fresh baby spinach

Directions:
1. Preheat the oven to 350°F.
2. Lightly spray an 8-by-8-inch baking dish with cooking spray and set aside.
3. Warm the olive oil in a medium skillet over medium-high heat. Sauté the carrots, onions, mushrooms, and garlic until softened, 5 to 6 minutes.
4. Whisk in the flour and cook for about 30 seconds. The mixture will thicken and look like a paste.
5. Stir in the soy milk and continue whisking until the sauce is thick, 3 to 4 minutes.
6. Whisk in the nutmeg and season the sauce with salt and pepper.
7. Place the quinoa and spinach in a medium bowl, pour in the sauce, and mix well to combine.
8. Spoon the mixture into the baking dish and bake until the casserole is lightly browned and heated through, about 15 minutes.
9. Serve.

Nutrition Info:
- Info Per Serving: Calories: 471 ; Fat: 12 g ;Saturated fat: 2 g ;Sodium: 103 mg

Ratatouille

Servings: 6
Cooking Time: X
Ingredients:
- 3 tablespoons olive oil
- 2 onions, chopped
- 4 cloves garlic, minced
- 1 green bell pepper, sliced
- 1 yellow bell pepper, sliced
- 1 eggplant, peeled and cubed
- ¼ teaspoon salt
- 1/8 teaspoon pepper
- 2 tablespoons flour
- 2 zucchini, sliced
- 1 tablespoon red-wine vinegar
- 2 tablespoons capers, rinsed
- ¼ cup chopped flat-leaf parsley

Directions:
1. In large saucepan, heat olive oil over medium heat. Add onion and garlic; cook and stir until crisp-tender, about 3 minutes. Add bell peppers; cook and stir until crisp-tender, about 3 minutes.
2. Sprinkle eggplant with salt, pepper, and flour. Add to saucepan; cook and stir until eggplant begins to soften. Add remaining ingredients except parsley; cover, and simmer for 30–35 minutes or until vegetables are soft and mixture is blended. Sprinkle with parsley and serve.

Nutrition Info:
- Info Per Serving: Calories:124.26; Fat:7.10 g ;Saturated fat:1.02 g ;Sodium: 187.22 mg

Kidney Bean Stew

Servings: 4
Cooking Time: 25 Min
Ingredients:
- 2 tsp avocado oil
- 1 leek, thinly sliced
- ½ brown onion, finely chopped
- 1 tsp garlic, minced
- 3 cups low-sodium vegetable stock
- 1 cup Roma tomatoes, chopped
- 2 medium carrots, peeled and thinly sliced
- 1 cup cauliflower florets
- 1 cup broccoli florets
- 1 green bell pepper, seeds removed and diced
- 1 cup low-sodium canned kidney beans, rinsed and drained
- Pinch red pepper flakes
- Himalayan pink salt
- Ground black pepper
- 2 tbsp. low-fat Parmesan cheese, grated for garnish
- 1 tbsp. parsley, chopped for garnish

Directions:

1. In a large-sized stockpot, warm the avocado oil over medium-high heat.

2. Add the sliced leek, chopped onions, and minced garlic and fry for 4 minutes until softened.

3. Add the vegetable stock, tomatoes, carrots, cauliflower, broccoli, green bell peppers, kidney beans, and red pepper flakes, mix to combine.

4. Bring the stew to a boil, then reduce the heat to low and simmer for 18 to 20 minutes until the vegetables are tender.

5. Season with salt and pepper to taste.

6. Top with Parmesan cheese and parsley.

Nutrition Info:

- Info Per Serving: Calories:270 ; Fat: 8g ;Saturated fat: 3g ;Sodium: 237 mg

Roasted Garlic Soufflé

Servings: 4
Cooking Time: X
Ingredients:

- 1 head Roasted Garlic
- 2 tablespoons olive oil
- 1 cup finely chopped cooked turkey breast
- ¼ cup grated Parmesan cheese
- 1/8 teaspoon pepper
- 1 egg
- ¼ cup low-fat sour cream
- 6 egg whites
- ¼ teaspoon cream of tartar
- ¼ cup chopped flat-leaf parsley

Directions:

1. Preheat oven to 375ºF. Grease the bottom of a 2-quart soufflé dish with peanut oil and set aside. Squeeze the garlic from the papery skins. Discard skins, and in medium bowl, combine olive oil with the garlic. Add turkey, cheese, pepper, egg, and sour cream, and mix well.

2. In large bowl, combine egg whites with cream of tartar. Beat until stiff peaks form. Stir a spoonful of egg whites into the turkey mixture and stir well. Then fold in remaining egg whites. Fold in parsley.

3. Spoon mixture into prepared soufflé dish. Bake for 40–50 minutes or until the soufflé is puffed and golden. Serve immediately.

Nutrition Info:

- Info Per Serving: Calories:223.79 ; Fat: 14.23 g ;Saturated fat:3.92 g ;Sodium: 253.37 mg

Chili-sautéed Tofu With Almonds

Servings: X
Cooking Time: 15 Minutes
Ingredients:

- 2 teaspoons olive oil
- ½ jalapeño pepper, chopped
- 1 teaspoon grated fresh ginger
- 1 teaspoon minced garlic
- 12 ounces extra-firm tofu, drained and cut into
- 1-inch cubes
- 2 cups shredded bok choy
- 1 red bell pepper, thinly sliced
- 1 scallion, white and green parts, thinly sliced
- 1 tablespoon low-sodium tamari sauce
- 1 tablespoon freshly squeezed lime juice
- 1 cup cooked quinoa, for serving
- ¼ cup chopped almonds, for garnish

Directions:

1. In a large skillet, warm the olive oil over medium-high heat.

2. Add the jalapeño, ginger, and garlic and sauté until softened, about 4 minutes.

3. Add the tofu, bok choy, bell peppers, and scallions and sauté until the tofu is lightly browned and the vegetables are tender, 8 to 10 minutes.

4. Stir in the tamari sauce and lime juice and toss to coat the ingredients.

5. Serve over quinoa, topped with chopped almonds.

Nutrition Info:

- Info Per Serving: Calories: 469 ; Fat: 24 g ;Saturated fat: 2 g ;Sodium: 279 mg

Salad Sandwich

Servings: 2
Cooking Time: 15 Min
Ingredients:

- 2 tsp apple cider vinegar
- 1 tsp avocado oil
- ¼ tsp ground cumin
- ¼ tsp wholegrain mustard
- ⅓ cup carrot, grated
- 2 tbsp. hummus, divided
- 4 slices wholegrain multigrain bread
- ½ ripe avocado, sliced
- 6 (½-inch-thick) jarred roasted red peppers, drained well
- 4 iceberg lettuce leaves

Directions:

1. In a small-sized mixing bowl, add the apple cider vinegar, avocado oil, cumin, and mustard, whisk to combine. Add the carrot and toss to coat and marinate for 10 minutes.

2. Spread the hummus on each slice of bread.

3. Divide the avocado slices between the two sandwiches. Top with peppers and lettuce.

4. Drain the marinaded carrots and add them on top of the lettuce. Close the sandwiches and enjoy.

Nutrition Info:

- Info Per Serving: Calories: 384 ; Fat: 16 g ;Saturated fat: 2 g ;Sodium: 463 mg

Crisp Polenta With Tomato Sauce

Servings: 8
Cooking Time: X

Ingredients:

- 1 recipe Cheese Polenta
- 1 cup shredded part-skim mozzarella cheese
- 3 cups Spaghetti Sauce , heated

Directions:

1. Prepare polenta as directed, except when done, pour onto a greased cookie sheet; spread to a ½"-thick rectangle, about 9″ × 15″. Cover and chill until very firm, about 2 hours.

2. Preheat broiler. Cut polenta into fifteen 3″ squares. Place on broiler pan; broil for 4–6 minutes or until golden brown. Carefully turn polenta and broil for 3–5 minutes or until golden brown.

3. Remove from oven and sprinkle with mozzarella cheese. Top each with a dollop of the hot Spaghetti Sauce, and serve immediately.

Nutrition Info:

- Info Per Serving: Calories: 229.70 ; Fat:8.43 g ;Saturated fat: 4.20 g ;Sodium: 260.08 mg

Pinto Bean Tortillas

Servings: 4
Cooking Time: 25 Min

Ingredients:

- 1 (15 oz) can low-sodium pinto beans, rinsed and drained
- ¼ cup canned fire-roasted tomato salsa
- ¾ cup dairy-free cheddar cheese, shredded and divided
- 1 medium red bell pepper, seeded, chopped and divided
- 2 tbsp. olive oil, divided
- 4 large, wholegrain tortillas

Directions:

1. Place the drained pinto beans and the tomato salsa together in a food processor. Process until smooth.

2. Spread ½ cup of the pinto bean mixture on each tortilla. Sprinkle each tortilla with 3 tbsp. of dairy-free cheddar cheese and ¼ cup of red bell pepper. Fold in half and repeat with the remaining tortillas.

3. Add 1 tbsp. of olive oil to a large, heavy-bottom pan over medium heat until hot. Place the first two folded tortillas in the pan. Cover and cook for 2 minutes until the tortillas are crispy on the bottom. Flip and cook for 2 minutes until crispy on the other side.

4. Repeat with the remaining folded tortillas and the remaining olive oil. Keep warm until ready to serve.

Nutrition Info:

- Info Per Serving: Calories:438 ; Fat: 21 g ;Saturated fat: 5 g ;Sodium: 561 mg

Tofu And Root Vegetable Curry

Servings: X
Cooking Time: 25 Minutes

Ingredients:

- 2 teaspoons olive oil
- 1 cup small cauliflower florets
- 1 parsnip, diced
- 1 carrot, diced
- 1 red bell pepper, thinly sliced
- 1 cup diced sweet potato
- 1 teaspoon peeled, grated fresh ginger
- ½ teaspoon minced garlic
- 1 cup low-sodium vegetable broth
- 2 tomatoes, chopped
- 2 cups diced extra-firm tofu
- 2 tablespoons curry powder or paste
- ¼ cup chopped cashews, for garnish

Directions:

1. In a large saucepan, warm the olive oil over medium-high heat.

2. Add the cauliflower, parsnips, carrots, bell peppers, sweet potatoes, ginger, and garlic and sauté until the vegetables begin to soften, about 10 minutes.

3. Stir in the vegetable broth, tomatoes, tofu, and curry powder and bring the mixture to a boil.

4. Reduce the heat to low and simmer until the vegetables are tender and everything is completely heated through, 15 to 18 minutes.

5. Serve topped with cashews.

Nutrition Info:

- Info Per Serving: Calories: 457 ; Fat: 20 g ;Saturated fat: 3 g ;Sodium: 135 mg

Portobello Burgers

Servings: 4
Cooking Time: 25 Min

Ingredients:

- Aluminium foil
- 3 tbsp. avocado oil
- 1 tbsp. garlic, crushed
- 4 large portobello mushrooms, stems removed
- 4 crusty whole-grain rolls
- ½ cup dairy-free cheddar cheese, shredded
- Ground black pepper
- 4 iceberg lettuce leaves

Directions:

1. Heat the oven to 425°F gas mark 7. Line a baking sheet with aluminum foil.
2. In a small-sized mixing bowl, add the avocado oil and garlic, mix to combine. Brush half of the garlic mixture on both sides of the portobello mushrooms and let them sit for 10 minutes.
3. Meanwhile, cut the rolls open. Drizzle the remaining garlic mixture onto the bottom half of each roll. Place 2 tbsp. of cheddar cheese on each bottom half roll.
4. Place the mushrooms on the prepared baking sheet, cap-side down, and roast for 12 minutes on each side.
5. Put one portobello mushroom on the bottom of each roll, on top of the cheddar cheese. Season with ground black pepper and top with 1 lettuce leaf. Place the top bun on the lettuce leaf and serve. Repeat for the remaining mushrooms.

Nutrition Info:

- Info Per Serving: Calories: 307 ; Fat: 17 g ;Saturated fat: 5 g ;Sodium: 276 mg

Stuffed Mushrooms

Servings: 4
Cooking Time: 10 Min
Ingredients:

- 4 large portobello mushrooms, stems removed
- 1 tbsp. avocado oil
- 1 (15 oz) can low-sodium garbanzo beans, drained and rinsed
- 1 cup wild rice, cooked
- ½ medium red bell pepper, seeds removed and finely chopped
- ½ cup red cabbage, finely chopped
- Himalayan pink salt
- Ground black pepper

Directions:
1. Heat the oven to 350°F gas mark 4.
2. Place the portobello mushrooms gill side down on a large baking sheet and drizzle with avocado oil.
3. Bake for 10 minutes, flip, and bake for another 10 minutes, until tender. Remove and leave the oven on.
4. In a large-sized mixing bowl, add the garbanzo beans, wild rice, red bell pepper, and red cabbage, season with salt and pepper to taste.
5. Divide the mixture into each portobello mushroom cup. Return to the oven and bake for 10 minutes until heated through. Remove from the oven and serve warm.

Nutrition Info:

- Info Per Serving: Calories: 194 ; Fat: 6 g ;Saturated fat: 1 g ;Sodium: 181 mg

Quinoa-stuffed Peppers

Servings: 6
Cooking Time: X
Ingredients:

- 1 recipe Quinoa Pepper Pilaf
- ½ cup chopped flat-leaf parsley
- 1 cup shredded Havarti cheese
- 6 large red bell peppers
- 2 cups Spaghetti Sauce

Directions:
1. Preheat oven to 350ºF. Prepare pilaf and fluff. Stir in parsley and Havarti. Cut tops from peppers and remove seeds and membranes.
2. Spray 9″ × 13″ baking dish with nonstick cooking spray. Place a layer of Spaghetti Sauce in the dish. Stuff peppers with pilaf and arrange on sauce. Pour remaining sauce over and around peppers.
3. Bake for 50–60 minutes or until peppers are tender. Serve immediately.

Nutrition Info:

- Info Per Serving: Calories: 406.04 ; Fat:15.40 g ;Saturated fat: 4.69 g ;Sodium: 468.06 mg

Chickpeas In Lettuce Wraps

Servings: 6–8
Cooking Time: X
Ingredients:

- 1 (15-ounce) can no-salt chickpeas
- 3 tablespoons olive oil
- 3 tablespoons lemon juice
- 3 cloves garlic, minced
- 1 tablespoon chopped fresh mint
- ½ cup diced red onion
- 8 lettuce leaves
- 1 cup chopped tomatoes
- 1 cup chopped yellow bell pepper

Directions:
1. Drain the chickpeas; rinse, and drain again. Place half in a blender or food processor. Add olive oil, lemon juice, garlic, and mint. Blend or process until smooth.
2. Place in medium bowl and stir in remaining chickpeas and red onion; stir until combined.
3. To make sandwiches, place lettuce leaves on work surface. Divide chickpea mixture among leaves and top with tomatoes and bell pepper. Roll up, folding in sides, to enclose filling. Serve immediately.

Nutrition Info:

- Info Per Serving: Calories:148.96; Fat:6.56 g ;Saturated fat:0.87 g ;Sodium: 6.80 g

Southwestern Millet-stuffed Tomatoes

Servings: X
Cooking Time: 25 Minutes
Ingredients:
- 4 large tomatoes
- ¼ teaspoon sea salt
- 2 teaspoon olive oil
- 1 sweet onion, chopped
- 1 orange bell pepper, chopped
- 2 small zucchini, chopped
- ½ jalapeño pepper, finely chopped
- 1 teaspoon minced garlic
- 2 cups cooked millet
- 1 cup fresh or frozen corn kernels (thawed, if frozen)
- Juice of ½ lime
- ¼ cup grated Parmesan cheese
- 2 teaspoons chopped fresh cilantro, for garnish

Directions:
1. Preheat the oven to 350°F.
2. Cut the tops off the tomatoes and discard. Carefully scoop out the insides of the tomatoes, leaving the shells intact. Sprinkle the inside of the tomatoes with salt and turn them upside down on paper towels to drain for about 15 minutes.
3. While the tomatoes are draining, warm the olive oil in a large skillet over medium-high heat.
4. Add the onions, bell peppers, zucchini, jalapeño, and garlic and sauté until softened, about 5 minutes.
5. Stir in the millet, corn, and lime juice and sauté until warm, 5 to 6 minutes.
6. Place the tomatoes, hollow-side up, in a medium baking dish.
7. Divide the millet mixture evenly among the tomatoes and top with the Parmesan cheese. Bake for approximately 15 minutes, or until the filling is completely heated through and the tomatoes are softened.
8. Serve topped with cilantro.

Nutrition Info:
- Info Per Serving: Calories: 464 ; Fat: 10 g ;Saturated fat: 2 g ;Sodium: 413 mg

Butternut Squash, Bulgur, And Tempeh Burritos

Servings: X
Cooking Time: 15 Minutes
Ingredients:
- 1 teaspoon olive oil
- 1 cup chopped butternut squash
- ½ cup chopped onion
- ½ cup cooked bulgur
- ½ cup crumbled tempeh

- ½ teaspoon chili powder
- ¼ teaspoon ground cumin
- 4 (6-inch) whole-grain tortillas
- ½ cup low-sodium tomato or mango salsa
- 1 scallion, white and green parts, sliced
- ½ cup shredded lettuce
- ¼ cup fat-free sour cream

Directions:
1. In a medium skillet, warm the olive oil over medium-high heat.
2. Add the squash and onions and sauté until tender, 8 to 10 minutes.
3. Add the bulgur, tempeh, chili powder, and cumin and sauté until the bulgur is heated through, about 7 minutes.
4. Wrap the tortillas in a clean kitchen towel and heat in the microwave for 15 to 30 seconds.
5. Lay the tortillas out and evenly divide the squash mixture between them. Top each with the salsa, scallion, lettuce, and sour cream.
6. Wrap the tortillas around the filling and serve.

Nutrition Info:
- Info Per Serving: Calories: 423 ; Fat: 13 g ;Saturated fat: 2 g ;Sodium: 712 mg

Peanut-butter-banana Skewered Sammies

Servings: 4–6
Cooking Time: X
Ingredients:
- ½ cup natural no-salt peanut butter
- 8 slices Honey-Wheat Sesame Bread
- 2 bananas
- 2 tablespoons lime juice
- 2 tablespoons butter or margarine, softened

Directions:
1. Spread peanut butter on one side of each slice of bread. Slice bananas, and as you work, sprinkle with lime juice. Make sandwiches by putting the bananas on the peanut butter and combining slices.
2. Butter the outsides of the sandwiches. Heat grill and cook sandwiches until bread is crisp and golden brown. Remove from grill, cut into quarters, and skewer on wood or metal skewers. Serve immediately.

Nutrition Info:
- Info Per Serving: Calories:376.36; Fat:18.67 g ;Saturated fat: 5.57 g ;Sodium: 77.44 mg

Quinoa Pepper Pilaf

Servings: 6
Cooking Time: X
Ingredients:

- 2 tablespoons olive oil
- 2 Italian frying peppers, chopped
- 1 green bell pepper, chopped
- 1 red bell pepper, chopped
- 1 onion, chopped
- 4 garlic cloves, minced
- ¼ cup chopped sun-dried tomatoes
- 1/8 teaspoon salt
- 1/8 teaspoon white pepper
- 1¼ cups quinoa
- 2½ cups low-sodium vegetable broth

Directions:

1. In large saucepan, heat olive oil over medium heat. Add frying peppers, green bell pepper, red bell pepper, onion, and garlic; cook and stir until crisp-tender, about 4 minutes. Add sun-dried tomatoes, salt, pepper, and quinoa; cook and stir for 2 minutes.
2. Pour in 1½ cups broth and bring to a simmer. Reduce heat to medium low and cook, stirring frequently, until the broth is absorbed, about 7 minutes. Add remaining broth and cook, stirring frequently, until quinoa is tender. Cover and remove from heat; let stand for 5 minutes. Fluff with a fork and serve.

Nutrition Info:

- Info Per Serving: Calories:241.29; Fat: 8.16 g ;Saturated fat: 1.14 g ;Sodium: 199.17 mg

Wild Rice & Lentils

Servings: 6
Cooking Time: 40 Min
Ingredients:

- 5 cups water
- 1 tsp sea salt, divided
- 1 cup wild rice
- 1 cup dried brown lentils, picked over
- ¼ cup olive oil
- 2 large brown onions, thinly sliced
- ½ cup cilantro, finely chopped
- 6 spring onions, thinly sliced, divided
- Ground black pepper

Directions:

1. In a large stockpot, add the water and add ¾ tsp salt, boil over high heat.
2. Add the rice and cook for 10 minutes, then lower the heat to a simmer.
3. Add the lentils and simmer. Cover the stockpot and reduce the heat to medium-low. Cook for 20 to 25 minutes, or until the rice and lentils are fully cooked. Remove from the heat.

4. Drain any remaining liquid and rest for 10 minutes.
5. In a large, heavy-bottom pan, heat the olive oil over medium heat. Line a plate with paper towels.
6. Once the oil is hot, add the onions and cook for 20 to 25 minutes, or until nicely browned, stirring frequently. Use a slotted spoon to transfer the onions onto the lined plate. Sprinkle with the remaining ¼ tsp salt.
7. Mix half of the onions, cilantro, and half the spring onion into the lentil and rice mixture.
8. Serve the lentil and rice in bowls and garnish with the remaining onions, spring onion, and pepper. Serve warm.

Nutrition Info:

- Info Per Serving: Calories: 333 ; Fat: 10 g ;Saturated fat: 7 g ;Sodium: 399 mg

Potato Soufflé

Servings: 4
Cooking Time: X
Ingredients:

- 2 Yukon Gold potatoes
- 1 tablespoon olive oil
- 1/8 teaspoon nutmeg
- ¼ teaspoon onion salt
- 1/8 teaspoon cayenne pepper
- 1/3 cup fat-free half-and-half
- ¼ cup grated Parmesan cheese
- 4 egg whites
- ¼ teaspoon cream of tartar
- 1 cup chopped grape tomatoes
- ¼ cup chopped fresh basil

Directions:

1. Preheat oven to 450ºF. Peel and thinly slice potatoes, adding to a pot of cold water as you work. Bring potatoes to a boil over high heat, reduce heat, and simmer until tender, about 12–15 minutes.
2. Drain potatoes and return to hot pot; shake for 1 minute. Add olive oil, nutmeg, salt, and pepper and mash until smooth. Beat in the half-and-half and Parmesan.
3. In large bowl, combine egg whites with cream of tartar and beat until stiff peaks form. Stir a dollop of the egg whites into the potato mixture and stir. Then fold in remaining egg whites.
4. Spray the bottom of a 2-quart casserole with nonstick cooking spray. Spoon potato mixture into casserole. Bake for 20 minutes, then reduce heat to 375ºF and bake for another 12–17 minutes or until soufflé is golden brown and puffed.
5. While soufflé is baking, combine tomatoes and basil in small bowl and mix gently. Serve immediately with tomato mixture for topping the soufflé.

Nutrition Info:

- Info Per Serving: Calories: 224.39; Fat:9.11 g ;Saturated fat:2.24 g ;Sodium: 260.97 mg

Stuffed Noodle Squash

Servings: 4
Cooking Time: 50 Min
Ingredients:
- 2 small spaghetti squash, halved lengthwise and seeds removed
- 1 cup water
- Aluminum foil
- 2 tbsp. olive oil
- 2 cups spinach, stems removed and finely chopped
- 1 cup chayote squash, peeled and chopped
- 1 cup canned garbanzo bean, drained and rinsed
- ¼ tsp fine sea salt
- ¼ tsp ground black pepper
- 1 cup Marinara Sauce

Directions:
1. Heat the oven to 400°F gas mark 6.
2. Place the spaghetti squashes cut side down on a large baking sheet.
3. Add the water to the baking sheet and cover it with aluminum foil. Bake for 35 to 40 minutes, or until the squash is fully cooked. Remove from the oven, leaving the oven on.
4. In a large, heavy-bottom pan, heat the olive oil over a medium heat.
5. Add the spinach and fry for 2 to 3 minutes until wilted.
6. Add the chayote squash and garbanzo beans, cook for 2 minutes until heated through.
7. Use a fork to scrape the flesh from the squash to remove the strands. Keep the shells.
8. Mix the strands into the garbanzo beans mixture and season with salt and pepper. Divide the mixture into the squash shells.
9. Drizzle each shell with ¼ cup Marinara Sauce. Return the stuffed squash to the oven and bake for 10 minutes until heated through. Serve hot.

Nutrition Info:
- Info Per Serving: Calories: 252 ; Fat: 13 g ;Saturated fat: 2 g ;Sodium: 330 mg

Cheese-and-veggie Stuffed Artichokes

Servings: 4
Cooking Time: X
Ingredients:
- 1 cup shredded Havarti cheese
- 2 tablespoons grated Parmesan cheese
- ¼ cup plain yogurt
- ¼ cup low-fat mayonnaise
- 1 tablespoon lemon juice
- 2 scallions, chopped
- 1 tablespoon capers
- 1 cup grated carrots
- 1 cup grape tomatoes
- 1/8 teaspoon salt
- 4 globe artichokes
- 1 lemon, cut into wedges

Directions:
1. In medium bowl, combine Havarti, Parmesan, yogurt, mayonnaise, lemon juice, scallions, and capers and mix well. Stir in carrots, tomatoes, and salt, and set aside.
2. Cut off the top inch of the artichokes. Cut off the sharp tip of each leaf. Pull off the tough outer leaves and discard. Rub cut edges with lemon wedges. Cut artichokes in half lengthwise.
3. Bring a large pot of salted water to a boil and add lemon wedges. Add artichokes and simmer for 20–25 minutes or until a leaf pulls out easily from the artichoke. Cool, then carefully remove choke with spoon.
4. Stuff artichokes with the cheese mixture, place on serving plate, cover, and chill for 2–4 hours before serving.

Nutrition Info:
- Info Per Serving: Calories: 266.61; Fat:14.24 g ;Saturated fat:6.47 g ;Sodium: 413.37 mg

Spanish Omelet

Servings: 4
Cooking Time: X
Ingredients:
- 2 tablespoons olive oil, divided
- 1 onion, minced
- 2 cloves garlic, minced
- 1 stalk celery, chopped
- ½ cup chopped red bell pepper
- 1 jalapeño pepper, minced
- ½ teaspoon dried oregano
- 2 tomatoes, chopped
- 1/8 teaspoon salt
- 1/8 teaspoon pepper
- 1 egg
- 8 egg whites
- ¼ cup skim milk
- 2 tablespoons low-fat sour cream
- ½ cup grated extra-sharp Cheddar cheese

Directions:
1. For the sauce, in a small saucepan heat 1 tablespoon olive oil over medium heat. Add onion, garlic, celery, bell pepper, and jalapeño pepper; cook and stir for 4 minutes until crisp-tender. Add oregano, tomatoes, salt, and pepper, and bring to a simmer. Reduce heat to low and simmer for 5 minutes.
2. In large bowl, combine egg, egg whites, skim milk, and sour cream and beat until combined. Heat 1 tablespoon olive oil in nonstick skillet and add egg mixture. Cook, moving

spatula around pan and lifting to let uncooked mixture flow underneath, until eggs are set but still moist.

3. Sprinkle with Cheddar and top with half of the tomato sauce. Cover and cook for 2–4 minutes longer, until bottom of omelet is golden brown. Fold over, slide onto serving plate, top with remaining tomato sauce, and serve.

Nutrition Info:

*   Info Per Serving: Calories: 219.98; Fat:14.03 g ;Saturated fat: 4.95 g ;Sodium: 316.92 mg

Cannellini Bean–stuffed Sweet Potatoes

Servings: X
Cooking Time: 25 Minutes
Ingredients:

*   2 large sweet potatoes
*   1 teaspoon olive oil
*   1 cup low-sodium canned white cannellini beans, rinsed and drained
*   1 red bell pepper, chopped
*   ½ cup chopped sweet onion
*   1 teaspoon minced garlic
*   1 cup shredded kale
*   1 tomato, chopped
*   1 teaspoon chopped fresh basil
*   ½ teaspoon chopped fresh oregano
*   Sea salt
*   Freshly ground black pepper
*   2 tablespoons roasted pumpkin seeds, for garnish

Directions:

1. Preheat the oven to 350°F.
2. Pierce the sweet potatoes with a fork and place them in an 8-by-8-inch baking dish. Bake until tender, about 45 minutes.
3. While the potatoes are baking, warm the olive oil in a medium skillet over medium-high heat. Add the cannellini beans, bell peppers, onions, and garlic and sauté until heated through and tender, about 10 minutes.
4. Stir in the kale, tomatoes, basil, and oregano and sauté until the greens are wilted, about 3 minutes.
5. Season the bean mixture with salt and pepper.
6. Cut each baked potato in half lengthwise from end to end. Scoop out about half of the sweet potato flesh, reserving it for use in another meal or recipe. Spoon the bean mixture into the potatoes.
7. Serve topped with pumpkin seeds.

Nutrition Info:

*   Info Per Serving: Calories: 406 ; Fat: 11 g ;Saturated fat: 2 g ;Sodium: 96 mg

Homestyle Bean Soup

Servings: 6
Cooking Time: 20 Min
Ingredients:

*   6 cups low-sodium vegetable stock
*   2 (15 oz) cans low-sodium kidney beans, drained and rinsed
*   1 (16 oz) can pinto beans, drained and rinsed
*   1 (15 oz) can diced tomatoes with their juices
*   ½ tsp Italian seasoning
*   1 cup carrots, finely chopped
*   1 cup celery stalk, finely chopped
*   Himalayan pink salt
*   Ground black pepper

Directions:

1. In a large-sized stockpot, add the vegetable stock, kidney beans, pinto beans, tomatoes in their juice, Italian seasoning, carrots, and celery, mix to combine.
2. Bring to a simmer over medium heat. Cook for 15 minutes, or until heated through. Remove from the heat and season with salt and pepper to taste. Serve hot.

Nutrition Info:

*   Info Per Serving: Calories: 238 ; Fat: 1 g ;Saturated fat: 0 g ;Sodium: 135 mg

Savory French Toast

Servings: 4–6
Cooking Time: X
Ingredients:

*   1 tablespoon olive oil
*   1 tablespoon butter
*   1 onion, chopped
*   4 (1-inch thick) slices Light Whole-Grain Bread
*   1 cup shredded Jarlsberg cheese
*   1 egg
*   1 egg white
*   1/3 cup buttermilk
*   1 teaspoon dried thyme leaves
*   ½ teaspoon hot sauce
*   1 cup Spaghetti Sauce

Directions:

1. In large saucepan, combine olive oil and butter over medium heat. Add onion; cook and stir until tender, about 5 minutes. Continue cooking until onion begins to turn golden, about 5–8 minutes longer. Remove onion from pan and place in small bowl. Remove pan from heat.
2. Let onion cool for 15 minutes. Meanwhile, cut a pocket in the center of each slice of bread. Add Jarlsberg to the onion mixture and mix. Stuff this into the bread pockets.
3. In shallow bowl, combine egg, egg whites, buttermilk, thyme, and hot sauce, and beat well. Dip stuffed bread into egg mixture, turning to coat.

4. Return saucepan to heat. Sauté the stuffed bread, turning once, about 4–5 minutes on each side until golden brown. Serve with the warmed Spaghetti Sauce.

Nutrition Info:
- Info Per Serving: Calories: 342.51 ; Fat: 14.56 g ;Saturated fat: 6.14 g ;Sodium: 198.74 mg

Spaghetti Squash Skillet

Servings: X
Cooking Time: 35 Minutes

Ingredients:
- 1 (2-pound) spaghetti squash
- 1 tablespoon olive oil, divided
- Sea salt
- Freshly ground black pepper
- ½ cup chopped sweet onion
- 1 teaspoon minced garlic
- 1 orange bell pepper, diced
- 16 asparagus spears, woody ends trimmed, cut into 2-inch pieces
- ½ cup sliced sun-dried tomatoes
- 2 cups shredded kale
- 1 tablespoon chopped fresh basil

Directions:
1. Preheat the oven to 400°F.
2. Line a baking sheet with parchment paper and set aside.
3. Slice the squash in half lengthwise and scoop out the seeds. Place the squash, cut-side up, on the baking sheet. Brush the cut edges and hollows with 1 teaspoon olive oil and season lightly with salt and pepper.
4. Roast the squash until a knife can be inserted easily into the thickest section, 30 to 35 minutes.
5. Remove from the oven and let the squash cool for 10 minutes, then use a fork to shred the flesh into a medium bowl. Set aside.

6. While the squash is cooling, warm the remaining 2 teaspoons olive oil in a medium skillet over medium heat. Add the onions and garlic and sauté until softened, about 3 minutes.
7. Stir in the bell pepper, asparagus, sun-dried tomatoes, and kale and sauté until the vegetables and greens are tender, about 5 minutes.
8. Add the shredded spaghetti squash and basil and toss to combine.
9. Serve.

Nutrition Info:
- Info Per Serving: Calories: 340 ; Fat:10 g ;Saturated fat: 2 g ;Sodium: 287 mg

Spaghetti With Creamy Tomato Sauce

Servings: 6–8
Cooking Time: X

Ingredients:
- 1 recipe Spaghetti Sauce
- ½ cup fat-free half-and-half
- 1 (16-ounce) package whole-grain pasta
- ½ cup grated Parmesan cheese

Directions:
1. Bring large pot of water to a boil. Prepare Spaghetti Sauce as directed. During last 5 minutes of cooking time, stir in light cream and stir to blend.
2. Cook pasta in boiling water according to package directions until al dente. Drain and add to Spaghetti Sauce; cook and stir for 1 minute to let the pasta absorb some of the sauce. Sprinkle with Parmesan and serve immediately.

Nutrition Info:
- Info Per Serving: Calories: 354.63; Fat:6.65 g ;Saturated fat:1.90 g ;Sodium:188.68 mg

Soups, Salads, And Sides

White Bean, Sausage, And Escarole Soup

Servings: 6
Cooking Time: X
Ingredients:
- ¼ cup water
- 6 ounces Italian sweet turkey sausage
- 2 tablespoons olive oil
- 4 cloves garlic, minced
- 2 onions, chopped
- 2 (14-ounce) cans no-salt diced tomatoes, undrained
- 2 cups Beans for Soup , thawed
- 3 cups Low-Sodium Beef Broth
- 2 cups water
- 6 cups chopped escarole
- 1 teaspoon dried oregano
- 1 bunch parsley, chopped
- 1/3 cup grated Parmesan cheese

Directions:
1. Place sausage in soup pot over medium heat. Add ¼ cup water and bring to a simmer. Simmer sausage, turning occasionally, until water evaporates. Then cook sausage, turning frequently, until browned. Remove sausage from pot and discard drippings; do not wash pot. Cut sausage into ½" slices.
2. Add olive oil to pot and add garlic and onion. Cook and stir until tender, about 5 minutes. Add tomatoes and stir. Add beans to pot along with broth, water, escarole, and oregano. Simmer for 15–25 minutes until escarole is tender.
3. Add sausage and parsley to soup and simmer for 5 minutes. Serve each soup bowl with a sprinkling of Parmesan cheese.

Nutrition Info:
- Info Per Serving: Calories:282.43 ; Fat:8.20 g ;Saturated fat:1.46 g ;Sodium: 267.96 mg

Baby Artichokes Stuffed With Tuna

Servings: 12
Cooking Time: X
Ingredients:
- 1 lemon
- 9 baby artichokes
- 8 cups water
- 1 (6-ounce) can white albacore tuna, drained
- 1 slice Honey-Wheat Sesame Bread , crumbled
- 2 shallots, minced
- 1 teaspoon fresh oregano
- 1/3 cup grated Parmesan cheese
- 3 tablespoons olive oil, divided

Directions:
1. Cut the lemon in half and squeeze the juice. Place half of the juice in a large bowl filled with cold water. Prepare artichokes by pulling off the outer leaves until you reach yellow leaves. Cut off the stem. Cut off the top one-third of the artichoke and discard. As you work, drop the trimmed artichokes into the bowl of lemon water.
2. In large pot, combine cold water and the squeezed lemon halves. Bring to a boil. Add the artichokes and bring back to a boil. Cover, reduce heat, and simmer for 10–15 minutes or until artichokes are tender.
3. Meanwhile, in small bowl combine drained tuna, breadcrumbs, shallots, oregano, Parmesan cheese, and 2 tablespoons olive oil and mix well.
4. When artichokes are tender, drain well. Cut artichokes in half and remove the choke, if necessary. Fill each artichoke half with some of the tuna mixture.
5. Preheat broiler. Place filled artichokes, stuffed side up, on a broiler pan. Drizzle with more olive oil. Broil 6″ from heat for 4–7 minutes or until filling starts to sizzle. Serve immediately.

Nutrition Info:
- Info Per Serving: Calories:90.34; Fat:4.60 g ;Saturated fat:1.08 g ;Sodium: 90.88 mg

Sesame Spinach

Servings: 3
Cooking Time: 2 Minutes
Ingredients:
- ½ pound spinach leaves
- 1 teaspoon minced garlic
- ½ tablespoon sesame oil
- Sea salt
- Freshly ground black pepper
- Sesame seeds

Directions:
1. Place a medium stockpot filled three-quarters full of water over high heat and bring to a boil.
2. Add the spinach and let boil for 1 to 2 minutes until softened.
3. Use a strainer to separate the spinach from the water and let cool. Then use your hands to squeeze out as much liquid from the spinach as possible.
4. Cut the spinach into bite-size pieces and transfer it to a medium bowl.
5. Add the garlic and sesame oil and season with salt and pepper.
6. Sprinkle with sesame seeds and serve immediately.

Nutrition Info:

- Info Per Serving: Calories: 56; Fat: 4 g ;Saturated fat: 1 g ;Sodium: 113 mg

Black-eyed Pea Salad

Servings: 6–8
Cooking Time: X
Ingredients:
- 1 (16-ounce) package dried black-eyed peas
- 8 cups cold water
- 1 cup plain yogurt
- ¼ cup olive oil
- ¼ cup Dijon mustard
- 1 teaspoon dried thyme leaves
- ¼ teaspoon salt
- 1/8 teaspoon pepper
- 2 green bell peppers, chopped
- 1 red bell pepper, chopped
- 1 red onion, finely chopped
- ½ cup crumbled goat cheese

Directions:
1. Pick over the peas and rinse; drain well, place in a large pot, cover with cold water, cover, and let stand overnight. In the morning, drain and rinse the peas and cover with cold water again. Bring to a boil, then reduce heat and simmer peas for 75–85 minutes until tender.
2. Meanwhile, in large bowl combine yogurt, olive oil, mustard, thyme, salt, and pepper and mix well. When peas are cooked, drain well and add to yogurt mixture along with peppers and red onion.
3. Toss gently to coat, then sprinkle with goat cheese. Cover and refrigerate for 4–6 hours before serving.

Nutrition Info:
- Info Per Serving: Calories:174.84 ; Fat:9.30 g ;Saturated fat:2.37 g ;Sodium: 212.18 mg

Creamy Vegetable Soup

Servings: 4
Cooking Time: 40 Min
Ingredients:
- 1 tsp olive oil
- 1 medium red onion, finely chopped
- 2 medium carrots, peeled and diced
- 2 cups courgettes, diced
- 1 small red potato, peeled and diced
- 1 cup dried green split peas
- 4 cups low-sodium vegetable stock
- ¼ tsp ground black pepper

Directions:
1. In a large stockpot, heat the olive oil over medium heat and add the onion and carrots. Cook for 5 minutes until the onions are translucent and the carrots are lightly browned.

2. Add the courgettes, red potato, split peas, vegetable stock, and pepper. Mix well and cook for 35 minutes on a low boil, partially covered.
3. Use an immersion blender and pulse 3 to 4 times until desired consistency. Serve hot.
Nutrition Info:
- Info Per Serving: Calories: 154; Fat: 2 g ;Saturated fat: 1 g ;Sodium: 178mg

Mixed Veg Salad

Servings: 4
Cooking Time: 10 Min
Ingredients:
- Aluminum foil
- 1 tbsp. olive oil, divided
- 1 large courgette, cut into thick julienne slices
- 2 medium carrots, peeled and cut into thick julienne slices
- 1 medium red bell pepper, seeded and cut into strips
- ½ small red onion, sliced
- 6 green asparagus spears, woody ends trimmed
- 2 cups cooked whole-grain Fusilli pasta
- ½ cup canned butter beans, rinsed and drained
- ½ cup grape tomatoes, halved
- 2 tbsp. sun-dried tomato and kalamata olive tapenade
- 1 tbsp. basil, chopped

Directions:
1. Preheat the oven broiler. Line a baking sheet with aluminum foil. Set aside.
2. In a medium-sized mixing bowl, add the olive oil, courgette, carrots, red bell pepper strips, red onion, and asparagus, mix well until the veggies are coated.
3. Place the vegetables on the baking sheet and broil for 6 to 8 minutes, or until the vegetables are al dente and slightly charred. Remove the vegetables and cool for 10 minutes.
4. Cut the asparagus into bite-size pieces.
5. Place the cooked vegetables in a medium-sized serving bowl and stir in the cooked pasta, butter beans, grape tomatoes, sun-dried tomato, and olive tapenade, and chopped basil, mix to coat.
6. Serve warm or cold.
Nutrition Info:
- Info Per Serving: Calories:433 ; Fat: 12g ;Saturated fat: 2g;Sodium:150mg

Cabbage-tomato-bean Chowder

Servings: 4
Cooking Time: X
Ingredients:

- 1 tablespoon olive oil
- 1 onion, chopped
- 4 cloves garlic, minced
- 3 cups shredded green cabbage
- 1 (14-ounce) can no-salt diced tomatoes, undrained
- 1 (6-ounce) can no-salt tomato paste
- 2 cups Low-Sodium Chicken Broth
- 1 teaspoon sugar
- 1/8 teaspoon white pepper
- 2 cups Beans for Soup
- 1/3 cup fat-free half-and-half

Directions:

1. In large saucepan, heat olive oil over medium heat. Add onion and garlic; cook and stir until crisp-tender, about 4 minutes. Add cabbage; cook and stir for 3 minutes longer.
2. Add tomatoes, tomato paste, chicken broth, sugar, and pepper. Cook and stir until tomato paste dissolves in soup. Then stir in beans and bring to a simmer. Simmer for 10 minutes, then add half-and-half. Heat until the soup steams, and serve.

Nutrition Info:

- Info Per Serving: Calories: 272.75 ; Fat: 4.96 g ;Saturated fat:0.95 g ;Sodium: 148.66 mg

Fried Tomatoes With Goat Cheese

Servings: 8
Cooking Time: X
Ingredients:

- 3 green tomatoes
- 1 egg
- ¼ cup buttermilk
- ½ cup cornmeal
- ¼ cup all-purpose flour
- 1 teaspoon baking powder
- 1/8 teaspoon cayenne pepper
- ½ cup olive oil
- 1/3 cup goat cheese

Directions:

1. Cut tomatoes into1/3 " slices; discard ends. In shallow bowl, combine egg and buttermilk and whisk to combine. On plate, combine cornmeal, flour, baking powder, and pepper and mix well.
2. Place olive oil in large saucepan over medium heat. When hot, dip tomato slices into egg mixture, then into cornmeal mixture to coat. Place carefully in oil and fry, turning once, until golden brown, about 3–5 minutes per side.
3. Drain fried tomatoes on paper towels and top each with a bit of goat cheese. Serve immediately.

Nutrition Info:

- Info Per Serving: Calories:127.27 ; Fat: 6.58g ;Saturated fat: 2.29g ;Sodium: 107.70 mg

Quinoa Vegetable Soup

Servings: 4
Cooking Time: 20 Minutes
Ingredients:

- 2 teaspoons olive oil
- 1 leek, white and light-green parts, chopped and rinsed
- 3 cloves garlic, minced
- 2 carrots, sliced ½-inch thick
- 3 cups low-sodium vegetable broth
- 2 tomatoes, chopped
- ¾ cup quinoa, rinsed and drained
- 1 sprig fresh rosemary
- 1 sprig fresh thyme
- Pinch salt
- ⅛ teaspoon cayenne pepper
- 1 cup baby spinach leaves

Directions:

1. In a large saucepan, heat the olive oil over medium heat.
2. Add the leek and garlic, and cook and stir for 2 minutes.
3. Add the carrot, broth, tomatoes, quinoa, rosemary, thyme, salt, and cayenne pepper, and bring to a simmer.
4. Reduce the heat to low, partially cover the pan, and simmer for 17 to 19 minutes, or until the vegetables and quinoa are tender. Stir in the spinach.
5. Remove the rosemary and thyme sprigs, and serve.

Nutrition Info:

- Info Per Serving: Calories:191 ; Fat: 6g ;Saturated fat: 1g ;Sodium:142 mg

Nuts On The Go

Servings: 3
Cooking Time: X
Ingredients:

- 1 cup unsalted mixed nuts
- ⅔ cup dried cranberries
- ½ cup coconut flakes, toasted
- ½ cup banana chips
- ¼ cup 60% dark chocolate chips (optional)

Directions:

1. Place the nuts, cranberries, coconut flakes, banana chips, and chocolate chips (if using) into an airtight container, mix to combine.
2. Keep for up to 1 week on the counter or for 3 months in the freezer.

Nutrition Info:

- Info Per Serving: Calories: 174 ; Fat:12 g ;Saturated fat: 2g ;Sodium: 18 mg

Greek Quesadillas

Servings: 8
Cooking Time: X
Ingredients:
- 1 cucumber
- 1 cup plain yogurt
- ½ teaspoon dried oregano leaves
- 1 tablespoon lemon juice
- ½ cup crumbled feta cheese
- 4 green onions, chopped
- 3 plum tomatoes, chopped
- 1 cup fresh baby spinach leaves
- 1 cup shredded part-skim mozzarella cheese
- 12 (6-inch) no-salt corn tortillas

Directions:
1. Peel cucumber, remove seeds, and chop. In small bowl, combine cucumber with yogurt, oregano, and lemon juice and set aside.
2. In medium bowl, combine feta cheese, green onions, tomatoes, baby spinach, and mozzarella cheese and mix well.
3. Preheat griddle or skillet. Place six tortillas on work surface. Divide tomato mixture among them. Top with remaining tortillas and press down gently.
4. Cook quesadillas, pressing down occasionally with spatula, until tortillas are lightly browned. Flip quesadillas and cook on second side until tortillas are crisp and cheese is melted. Cut quesadillas in quarters and serve with yogurt mixture.

Nutrition Info:
- Info Per Serving: Calories:181.26 ; Fat: 6.34 g ;Saturated fat:3.62 g ;Sodium: 208.14 mg

Lemony Green Beans With Almonds

Servings: 5
Cooking Time: 2 Minutes
Ingredients:
- 3 cups water
- 1 pound green beans, trimmed
- 1 cup diced carrots
- 1 red bell pepper, sliced
- ¼ cup slivered almonds
- ½ cup Lemon-Garlic Sauce

Directions:
1. In a medium pot over high heat, bring the water to a boil. Once the water is boiling, add the green beans and cook for 2 minutes, then drain the beans and run under cold water to cool them.
2. In a large bowl, combine the green beans, carrots, bell pepper, almonds, and Lemon-Garlic Sauce. Enjoy.

Nutrition Info:
- Info Per Serving: Calories: 133 ; Fat: 8 g ;Saturated fat: 1 g ;Sodium: 254 mg

Apple-carrot-kale Salad

Servings: 5
Cooking Time: 15 Minutes
Ingredients:
- 5 cups chopped kale
- 1 shredded Envy apple (or other apple of choice)
- ½ cup slivered almonds
- 1 cup shredded carrots
- ½ cup Lemon-Garlic Sauce

Directions:
1. In a large bowl, toss the together the kale, apple, almonds, and carrots.
2. Drizzle the Lemon-Garlic Sauce onto the salad and serve immediately.

Nutrition Info:
- Info Per Serving: Calories: 153 ; Fat: 11 g ;Saturated fat: 1 g ;Sodium: 255 mg

Caramelized Spiced Carrots

Servings: 6
Cooking Time: X
Ingredients:
- 1¼ pounds baby carrots
- ¼ cup orange juice
- 1/8 teaspoon salt
- 1/8 teaspoon white pepper
- 1 teaspoon grated orange zest
- 1 tablespoon sugar
- 1 tablespoon grated ginger root
- 1 tablespoon butter or plant sterol margarine

Directions:
1. In large saucepan, combine carrots, orange juice, salt, and pepper. Bring to a boil over high heat, then reduce heat to low, cover, and cook for 3–4 minutes or until carrots are crisp-tender.
2. Add orange zest, sugar, ginger root, and butter and bring to a boil over high heat. Cook until most of the orange juice evaporates and the carrots start to brown, stirring frequently, about 4–5 minutes. Serve immediately.

Nutrition Info:
- Info Per Serving: Calories: 62.66 ; Fat: 2.07 g ;Saturated fat: 1.24 g ;Sodium: 135.88 mg

Chili Fries

Servings: 4–6
Cooking Time: X
Ingredients:
- 4 russet potatoes
- 2 tablespoons olive oil
- 2 tablespoons chili powder
- 1 tablespoon grill seasoning
- 1 teaspoon ground cumin
- 1 teaspoon paprika

- ¼ teaspoon pepper

Directions:

1. Preheat oven to 425ºF. Scrub potatoes and pat dry; cut into ½" strips, leaving skin on. A few strips won't have any skin. Toss with olive oil and arrange in single layer on a large cookie sheet.

2. In small bowl, combine remaining ingredients and mix well. Sprinkle over potatoes and toss to coat. Arrange in single layer.

3. Bake for 35–45 minutes, turning once during baking time, until potatoes are deep golden brown and crisp. Serve immediately.

Nutrition Info:

- Info Per Serving: Calories:225.16; Fat: 4.76 g ;Saturated fat: 0.69 g;Sodium: 213.81 mg

Lime Brussels Sprouts

Servings: X
Cooking Time: 10 Minutes
Ingredients:

- 2 teaspoons olive oil
- 1 pound Brussels sprouts, quartered
- ¼ teaspoon minced garlic
- Juice and zest of 1 lime
- Sea salt
- Freshly ground black pepper

Directions:

1. In a medium skillet, warm the olive oil over medium-high heat.

2. Add the Brussels sprouts and garlic and sauté until tender, 5 to 6 minutes.

3. Stir in the lime juice and zest and sauté for 1 more minute.

4. Season with salt and pepper and serve.

Nutrition Info:

- Info Per Serving: Calories: 144 ; Fat: 6 g ;Saturated fat: 1 g ;Sodium: 81 mg

Tomato Sauce–simmered Eggplant

Servings: 5
Cooking Time: 20 Minutes
Ingredients:

- 1 medium eggplant, cut into 1-inch cubes
- ¾ cup Tasty Tomato Sauce
- 1 tablespoon olive oil
- 2 cups low-sodium canned diced tomatoes
- 2 bay leaves
- ½ cup water
- 1 tablespoon chopped fresh parsley

Directions:

1. In a large, deep skillet over medium-high heat, cook the eggplant, Tasty Tomato Sauce, and olive oil for 2 minutes, or until the eggplant is soft.

2. Add the tomatoes with their juices, bay leaves, and water to the eggplant mixture and simmer for 15 minutes, until fragrant.

3. Stir in the parsley.

4. Remove the bay leaves and serve immediately.

Nutrition Info:

- Info Per Serving: Calories: 111; Fat: 3 g ;Saturated fat: 0 g ;Sodium: 45 mg

Scalloped Potatoes With Aromatic Vegetables

Servings: 8
Cooking Time: X
Ingredients:

- 2 carrots, peeled and sliced
- 2 parsnips, peeled and sliced
- 3 russet potatoes, sliced
- ¼ cup olive oil
- 1/8 teaspoon salt
- 1/8 teaspoon white pepper
- 1 onion, finely chopped
- 4 cloves garlic, minced
- 1/3 cup grated Parmesan cheese
- ¼ cup dry breadcrumbs
- 1 cup milk

Directions:

1. Preheat oven to 375ºF. Spray a 9″ × 13″ baking dish with nonstick cooking spray and set aside.

2. In large bowl, combine carrots, parsnips, and potatoes; drizzle with olive oil, sprinkle with salt and pepper, and toss to coat. Layer vegetables in prepared baking dish, sprinkling each layer with onion, garlic, Parmesan, and breadcrumbs, finishing with breadcrumbs.

3. Pour milk into casserole. Cover tightly with foil. Bake for 45 minutes, then uncover. Bake for 15–25 minutes longer or until vegetables are tender and top is browned. Serve immediately.

Nutrition Info:

- Info Per Serving: Calories:271.60 ; Fat:9.04 g ;Saturated fat: 2.03 g;Sodium: 211.64 mg

Roasted-garlic Corn

Servings: 6
Cooking Time: X
Ingredients:

- 3 cups frozen corn, thawed
- 2 tablespoons olive oil
- 2 shallots, minced
- 1 head Roasted Garlic
- 1/8 teaspoon salt
- 1/8 teaspoon white pepper

Directions:

1. Preheat oven to 425°F. Place corn on paper towels and pat to dry. Place a Silpat liner on a 15″ × 10″ jelly-roll pan. Combine corn, olive oil, and shallots on pan and toss to coat. Spread in even layer.

2. Roast corn for 14–22 minutes, stirring once during cooking time, until kernels begin to turn light golden brown in spots.

3. Remove cloves from Roasted Garlic and add to corn along with salt and white pepper. Stir to mix, then serve.

Nutrition Info:
- Info Per Serving: Calories:147.64 ; Fat: 6.70 g ;Saturated fat: 0.94 g;Sodium: 79.60 mg

Indian Vegetable Soup

Servings: 2-4
Cooking Time: 25 Min
Ingredients:
- 1 tsp coconut oil
- ½ cup red onion, finely chopped
- 1 tsp garlic, crushed
- 1 tsp ginger, peeled and grated
- 1 small cauliflower head, roughly chopped
- 1 cup canned lentils, rinsed and drained
- 4 cups low-sodium vegetable broth
- 1 tbsp. mild curry powder
- Himalayan pink salt
- ¼ cup low-fat plain yoghurt
- 1 tsp parsley, chopped for garnish

Directions:
1. Heat the coconut oil in a large stockpot over medium-high heat.

2. Add the onion, garlic, and ginger, fry for 3 minutes until softened.

3. Mix in the cauliflower, lentils, vegetable broth, and curry powder, allow the mixture to boil.

4. Reduce the heat to low and simmer for 20 minutes until the cauliflower is tender.

5. Transfer the soup to a food processor and process until no lumps remain.

6. Pour the soup back into the stockpot and mix in the plain yoghurt.

7. Garnish with chopped parsley and serve hot.

Nutrition Info:
- Info Per Serving: Calories: 231 ; Fat: 3 g ;Saturated fat: 0 g ;Sodium: 141 mg

Spanish Garlic-lentil Soup

Servings: 6
Cooking Time: X
Ingredients:
- 1 cup lentils
- 3 cups Low-Sodium Beef Broth
- 3 cup water
- 4 slices Honey-Wheat Sesame Bread
- 2 tablespoons olive oil
- 1 head garlic, peeled and sliced
- 2 ounces chorizo sausage, thinly sliced
- 1/8 teaspoon cayenne pepper
- ¼ cup sliced almonds, toasted

Directions:
1. Pick over lentils and rinse; drain thoroughly. Place in large pot with the beef broth and water and bring to a simmer. Cover and simmer for 20–25 minutes or until lentils are tender.

2. Meanwhile, rub bread slices between your hands to make breadcrumbs. In another large saucepan, place the olive oil over medium heat. Add garlic, breadcrumbs, and sausage and cook, stirring frequently, until garlic is soft and breadcrumbs are toasted.

3. When lentils are tender, stir garlic mixture into broth along with cayenne pepper. Simmer for 5 minutes, then garnish with almonds and serve.

Nutrition Info:
- Info Per Serving: Calories: 338.34; Fat: 12.91 g ;Saturated fat: 3.02 g ;Sodium: 151.54 mg

Veggie-stuffed Tomatoes

Servings: 4
Cooking Time: X
Ingredients:
- 1 tablespoon olive oil
- 1 onion, chopped
- 3 cloves garlic, minced
- 1 green bell pepper, chopped
- 4 stalks celery, chopped
- 1 tablespoon chopped fresh chives
- 2 teaspoons fresh oregano leaves
- 1/8 teaspoon salt
- 1/8 teaspoon pepper
- ½ cup plain yogurt
- 1 tablespoon lime juice
- 2 tablespoons grated Parmesan cheese
- 4 large tomatoes

Directions:
1. In medium saucepan, heat olive oil over medium heat. Add onion, garlic, and green bell pepper; cook and stir until crisp-tender, about 4 minutes. Remove from heat and stir in

celery, chives, oregano, salt, and pepper. Remove to medium bowl and chill until cold, about 1 hour.

2. Stir yogurt, lime juice, and Parmesan into cooled vegetable mixture. Cut tops off tomatoes and gently scoop out tomato flesh and seeds, leaving a ½" shell. Stuff with the vegetable mixture. Cover and chill for 2–3 hours before serving.

Nutrition Info:

- Info Per Serving: Calories:122.14; Fat:5.75 g ;Saturated fat: 1.74 g;Sodium: 194.39 mg

Fried Green Tomatoes

Servings: 8
Cooking Time: X
Ingredients:

- 4 large green tomatoes
- 1 egg
- ¼ cup buttermilk
- ½ cup cornmeal
- ½ cup all-purpose flour
- 1 teaspoon baking powder
- 1/8 teaspoon white pepper
- ¼ cup canola oil

Directions:

1. Slice tomatoes into 1/3" rounds and pat dry with paper towels. In shallow bowl, combine egg and buttermilk and whisk until blended. On plate, combine cornmeal, flour, baking powder, and pepper and mix well.

2. Place oil in heavy skillet and place over medium heat until temperature reaches 375°F. Dip tomato slices into egg mixture, then into cornmeal mixture. Fry tomatoes in hot oil, four at a time, turning once, until golden brown, about 3–6 minutes per side. Drain on paper towels and serve immediately.

Nutrition Info:

- Info Per Serving: Calories:116.06 ; Fat: 3.64 g ;Saturated fat:0.47 g ;Sodium: 74.42 mg

Spiced Root Veggie

Servings: 1-2
Cooking Time: 10 Min
Ingredients:

- 1 tsp avocado oil
- ½ tsp garlic, crushed
- ½ tsp ginger, peeled and grated
- ¼ tsp ground cumin
- ⅛ tsp ground coriander
- 3 large carrots, peeled and thinly sliced
- ¼ cup low-sodium vegetable broth
- ½ lemon, juiced
- 1 tbsp. organic honey
- Himalayan pink salt
- Ground black pepper

Directions:

1. Warm the olive oil in a medium-sized stockpot over medium-high heat.

2. Add the garlic, ginger, cumin, and coriander and fry for 2 minutes until fragrant.

3. Mix in the carrots, vegetable broth, lemon juice, and honey. Boil the mixture, reduce the heat to low, and simmer for 6 to 8 minutes until the carrots are tender.

4. Season with salt and pepper, serve immediately.

Nutrition Info:

- Info Per Serving: Calories: 103 ; Fat:3 g ;Saturated fat: 0g ;Sodium: 86 mg

Tangy Fish And Tofu Soup

Servings: 5
Cooking Time: 10 Minutes
Ingredients:

- 1 pound white fish (such as tilapia), thinly sliced
- ⅓ cup Tangy Soy Sauce
- 8 cups water
- 4 cups chopped napa cabbage
- 1 white onion, chopped
- 12 ounces soft tofu, cubed

Directions:

1. Place the fish and the Tangy Soy Sauce in a resealable plastic bag. Place the bag in the refrigerator and let the fish marinate for 30 minutes.

2. Once marinated, bring the water to a boil in a large pot over high heat. Add the cabbage and onion and bring to a boil again.

3. Add the tofu, marinated fish, and any remaining marinade to the pot.

4. Bring the soup back to a boil, reduce the heat to medium, and simmer for 5 minutes, until fragrant. Serve immediately.

Nutrition Info:

- Info Per Serving: Calories :181 ; Fat: 4g ;Saturated fat: 1g ;Sodium: 271 mg

Thai Chicken Soup

Servings: 4
Cooking Time: 20 Minutes
Ingredients:

- 2 teaspoons olive oil
- 2 (6-ounce) boneless, skinless chicken breasts
- Pinch salt
- ⅛ teaspoon cayenne pepper
- 1 lemongrass stalk, peeled and chopped
- 4 cloves garlic, minced
- 1 jalapeño chile, seeded and minced
- 1 red bell pepper, seeded and chopped
- 2 cups low-sodium chicken stock
- 1 cup water
- 2 tablespoons fresh lime juice

- 1 teaspoon Thai chili paste
- ⅛ teaspoon ground ginger

Directions:

1. In a large saucepan, heat the olive oil over medium heat.
2. Sprinkle the chicken with the salt and cayenne pepper, and add it to the saucepan. Cook, turning once, until the chicken is browned, about 3 to 4 minutes per side. Transfer the chicken to a plate and set aside.
3. Add the lemongrass, garlic, jalapeño, and bell pepper to the saucepan, and cook for 3 minutes, stirring frequently.
4. Add the chicken stock and water to the saucepan, and stir and bring to a simmer. Return the chicken to the saucepan. Simmer for 10 to 12 minutes, or until the chicken is cooked to 165°F when tested with a meat thermometer.
5. Remove the chicken to a clean plate and shred, using two forks. Return the chicken to the soup.
6. Add the lime juice, chili paste, and ginger, and simmer for 2 minutes longer. Serve hot.

Nutrition Info:

- Info Per Serving: Calories: 134 ; Fat: 5 g ;Saturated fat: 1 g ;Sodium: 237 mg

Marinated Baby Artichokes

Servings: 4
Cooking Time: X
Ingredients:

- 1 lemon, cut in half
- 6 baby artichokes
- 8 cups water
- 1 teaspoon ground coriander
- 3 tablespoons extra-virgin olive oil
- 1 tablespoon Dijon mustard
- 1 shallot, peeled and minced
- 1/8 teaspoon pepper

Directions:

1. Cut the lemon in half and squeeze the juice. Place half of juice in large bowl filled with cold water. Prepare artichokes by pulling off outer leaves until you reach yellow leaves. Cut off stem. Cut off top one-third of artichoke and discard. As you work, drop trimmed artichokes into bowl of lemon water.
2. In large pot, combine cold water, ground coriander, and squeezed lemon halves. Bring to a boil. Add the artichokes and bring back to a boil. Cover, reduce heat, and simmer for 10–15 minutes or until artichokes are tender.
3. Meanwhile, in small bowl, combine remaining half of lemon juice, olive oil, mustard, shallot, and pepper, and whisk to blend.
4. When artichokes are tender, drain and rinse with cold water. Cut artichokes in quarters lengthwise. If necessary, with a spoon, carefully remove the prickly choke from the center. Arrange artichokes on serving plate and drizzle with olive oil mixture.

Nutrition Info:

- Info Per Serving: Calories: 129.79; Fat:10.39g ;Saturated fat:1.43 g ;Sodium: 100.09mg

Low-sodium Chicken Broth

Servings: 8
Cooking Time: X
Ingredients:

- 2 tablespoons olive oil
- 3 pounds cut-up chicken
- 2 onions, chopped
- 5 cloves garlic, minced
- 4 carrots, sliced
- 4 stalks celery, sliced
- 1 tablespoon peppercorns
- 1 bay leaf
- 6 cups water
- 2 tablespoons lemon juice

Directions:

1. In large skillet, heat olive oil over medium heat. Add chicken, skin-side down, and cook until browned, about 8–10 minutes. Place chicken in 5- to 6-quart slow cooker.
2. Add onions and garlic to drippings in skillet; cook and stir for 2–3 minutes, scraping bottom of skillet. Add to slow cooker along with remaining ingredients except lemon juice. Cover and cook on low for 8–9 hours.
3. Strain broth into large bowl. Remove meat from chicken; refrigerate or freeze for another use. Cover broth and refrigerate overnight. In the morning, remove fat solidified on surface and discard. Stir in lemon juice. Pour broth into freezer containers, seal, label, and freeze up to 3 months. To use, defrost in refrigerator overnight.

Nutrition Info:

- Info Per Serving: Calories: 82.89 ; Fat: 5.22g ;Saturated fat:0.92 mg;Sodium: 39.09 mg

Savory Chicken And Watermelon Rind Soup

Servings: 4
Cooking Time: 35 Minutes
Ingredients:

- 1 tablespoon olive oil
- ¾ pound boneless, skinless chicken thighs
- 2 tablespoons minced garlic
- 1 teaspoon peeled minced fresh ginger
- Pinch sea salt
- Pinch freshly ground black pepper
- 6 cups water
- 3 cups diced watermelon rind

Directions:

1. In a large stockpot, heat the olive oil over medium heat. Add the chicken, garlic, ginger, salt, and pepper, and sauté until the chicken is no longer pink, about 5 minutes.

2. Add the water to the pot, increase the heat to high, and bring the soup to a boil.

3. Add the watermelon rind once the water comes to a boil.

4. Allow the soup to come to a boil again, reduce the heat to medium, and simmer for 30 minutes.

5. Add more salt, if desired, and enjoy immediately.

Nutrition Info:

- Info Per Serving: Calories: 157 ; Fat: 7 g ;Saturated fat: 1g ;Sodium: 121 mg

Creamy Chicken And Corn Soup

Servings: 5

Cooking Time: 10 Minutes

Ingredients:

- 5¼ cups water, plus 2 tablespoons, divided
- 3 (14-ounce) cans low-sodium cream-style corn
- ½ pound skinless, boneless chicken breast, thinly sliced
- 1 cup liquid egg whites
- 3 tablespoons diced scallions, both green and white parts
- 1 teaspoon cornstarch
- Sea salt
- Freshly ground black pepper

Directions:

1. In a large stockpot, bring 5¼ cups of water to a boil over high heat.

2. Stir in the corn and return to a boil. Add the chicken and boil for 5 minutes.

3. Add the egg whites and scallions, reduce the heat to medium, and simmer for 5 minutes, until the egg whites turn opaque.

4. In a small bowl, mix the cornstarch with the remaining 2 tablespoons of water, then add it to the soup and stir until the soup thickens, about 1 or 2 minutes.

5. Season with salt and pepper and serve immediately.

Nutrition Info:

- Info Per Serving: Calories: 254 ; Fat: 2 g ;Saturated fat: 0g ;Sodium: 140 mg

Sauces, Dressings, And Staples

Smoky Barbecue Rub

Servings: ½
Cooking Time: X
Ingredients:
- 2 tablespoons smoked paprika
- 2 tablespoons brown sugar
- 1 tablespoon chili powder
- 1 tablespoon garlic powder
- 2 teaspoons onion powder
- 2 teaspoons celery salt
- 1 teaspoon ground cumin
- ½ teaspoon sea salt
- ½ teaspoon dried oregano

Directions:
1. In a small bowl, whisk together the paprika, sugar, chili powder, garlic powder, onion powder, celery salt, cumin, salt, and oregano until well blended.
2. Transfer to an airtight container to store.

Nutrition Info:
- Info Per Serving: Calories: 23 ; Fat: 1 g ;Saturated fat: 0 g ;Sodium: 113 mg

Spicy Peanut Sauce

Servings: 8
Cooking Time: 15 Minutes
Ingredients:
- ½ cup powdered peanut butter (see Ingredient Tip)
- 2 tablespoons reduced-fat peanut butter
- ⅓ cup plain nonfat Greek yogurt
- 2 tablespoons fresh lime juice
- 2 teaspoons low-sodium soy sauce
- 1 scallion, chopped
- 1 clove garlic, minced
- 1 jalapeño pepper, seeded and minced
- ⅛ teaspoon red pepper flakes

Directions:
1. In a blender or food processor, combine powdered peanut butter, reduced-fat peanut butter, yogurt, lime juice, soy sauce, scallion, garlic, jalapeño pepper, and red pepper flakes, and blend or process until smooth.
2. Serve immediately or store in an airtight glass container and refrigerate for up to 3 days. You can thin this sauce with more lime juice if necessary.

Nutrition Info:
- Info Per Serving: Calories: 60 ; Fat: 3 g ;Saturated fat: 0 g ;Sodium: 88 mg

Zesty Citrus Kefir Dressing

Servings: 8
Cooking Time: 15 Minutes
Ingredients:
- ⅔ cup kefir
- 2 tablespoons honey
- 2 tablespoons low-sodium yellow mustard
- 2 tablespoons fresh lemon juice
- ½ teaspoon fresh lemon zest
- 1 tablespoon fresh orange juice
- ½ teaspoon fresh orange zest
- 1 teaspoon olive oil
- Pinch salt

Directions:
1. In a blender or food processor, combine the kefir, honey, mustard, lemon juice and zest, orange juice and zest, olive oil, and salt. Blend or process until smooth.
2. You can serve this dressing immediately, or store it in an airtight container in the refrigerator for up to 3 days.

Nutrition Info:
- Info Per Serving: Calories: 37 ; Fat: 1 g ;Saturated fat: 0 g ;Sodium: 43 mg

Avocado Dressing

Servings: 8
Cooking Time: 15 Minutes
Ingredients:
- 1 avocado, peeled and cubed
- ⅔ cup plain nonfat Greek yogurt
- ¼ cup buttermilk
- 2 tablespoons fresh lemon juice
- 1 tablespoon honey
- Pinch salt
- 2 tablespoons chopped fresh chives
- ½ cup chopped cherry tomatoes

Directions:
1. In a blender or food processor, combine the avocado, yogurt, buttermilk, lemon juice, honey, salt, and chives, and blend or process until smooth. Stir in the tomatoes.
2. You may need to add more buttermilk or lemon juice to achieve a pourable consistency.
3. This dressing can be stored by putting it into a small dish, then pouring about 2 teaspoons lemon juice on top. Cover the dressing by pressing plastic wrap directly onto the surface. Refrigerate for up to 1 day.

Nutrition Info:
- Info Per Serving: Calories:55 ; Fat: 3g ;Saturated fat: 1g ;Sodium: 30mg

Chimichurri Sauce

Servings: 8
Cooking Time: 15 Minutes
Ingredients:
- 1 shallot, chopped
- 1 garlic clove, chopped
- ½ cup fresh flat-leaf parsley
- ½ cup fresh cilantro leaves
- 3 tablespoons fresh basil leaves
- 2 tablespoons fresh lemon juice
- 2 tablespoons low-sodium vegetable broth
- Pinch salt
- ⅛ teaspoon red pepper flakes

Directions:
1. In a blender or food processor, add the shallot, garlic, parsley, cilantro, basil, lemon juice, vegetable broth, salt, and red pepper flakes, and process until the herbs are in tiny pieces and the mixture is well-combined.
2. Serve immediately or store in an airtight glass container in the refrigerator up to 2 days. Stir the sauce before serving.

Nutrition Info:
- Info Per Serving: Calories: 5 ; Fat: 0 g ;Saturated fat: 0 g ;Sodium: 3 mg

Buttermilk-herb Dressing

Servings: ¾
Cooking Time: X
Ingredients:
- ½ cup buttermilk
- ¼ cup silken tofu
- 2 tablespoons minced scallion, white part only
- 1 tablespoon chopped fresh parsley
- 1 tablespoon chopped fresh thyme
- 1 teaspoon chopped fresh dill
- Sea salt
- Freshly ground black pepper

Directions:
1. In a medium bowl, whisk together the buttermilk, tofu, scallions, parsley, thyme, and dill until well blended.
2. Season with salt and pepper.

Nutrition Info:
- Info Per Serving: Calories: 17 ; Fat: 0 g ;Saturated fat: 0 g ;Sodium: 35 mg

Spinach And Walnut Pesto

Servings: 5
Cooking Time: X
Ingredients:
- 2 cups spinach
- ½ cup chopped walnuts
- ½ cup olive oil
- 2 tablespoons minced garlic
- ½ teaspoon salt

Directions:
1. In a blender, place the spinach, walnuts, olive oil, garlic, and salt and blend until smooth. Use immediately.

Nutrition Info:
- Info Per Serving: Calories: 275 ; Fat: 29 g ;Saturated fat: 4g ;Sodium: 243 mg

Mango, Peach, And Tomato Pico De Gallo

Servings: 4
Cooking Time: 15 Minutes
Ingredients:
- 1 mango, peeled and cubed (see Ingredient Tip)
- 1 peach, peeled and chopped (see Ingredient Tip)
- 1 beefsteak tomato, cored and chopped
- 1 cup yellow or red cherry tomatoes, chopped
- 2 scallions, chopped
- 1 jalapeño pepper, seeded and minced
- 2 tablespoons fresh lemon juice
- 1 teaspoon fresh grated lemon zest
- Pinch salt
- ⅛ teaspoon red pepper flakes

Directions:
1. In a medium bowl, combine the mango, peach, tomato, scallions, jalapeño pepper, lemon juice, lemon zest, salt, and red pepper flakes, and mix well.
2. Serve immediately or store in an airtight glass container in the refrigerator for up to 2 days.

Nutrition Info:
- Info Per Serving: Calories: 80 ; Fat: 1 g ;Saturated fat: 0 g ;Sodium: 48 mg

Sweet Potato And Navy Bean Hummus

Servings: X
Cooking Time: X
Ingredients:
- 1 cup mashed cooked sweet potato
- 1 cup low-sodium canned navy beans, rinsed and drained
- 2 tablespoons tahini
- 2 tablespoons olive oil
- Juice of 1 lime
- ½ teaspoon minced garlic
- ¼ teaspoon ground cumin
- Sea salt
- Chopped fresh cilantro, for garnish
- Pita bread, baked tortilla crisps, or veggies, for serving

Directions:
1. In a food processor or blender, add the sweet potato, beans, tahini, olive oil, lime juice, garlic, and cumin and

purée until very smooth, scraping down the sides at least once.

2. Season with salt, top with cilantro, and serve with pita bread, baked tortilla crisps, or veggies.

Nutrition Info:
- Info Per Serving: Calories: 396 ; Fat: 23 g ;Saturated fat: 3 g ;Sodium: 78 mg

Tofu-horseradish Sauce

Servings: X
Cooking Time: X
Ingredients:
- ¼ cup silken tofu
- 1 tablespoon prepared horseradish
- 1 tablespoon minced scallion, white part only
- 1 tablespoon chopped fresh parsley
- ½ teaspoon minced garlic
- Sea salt
- Freshly ground black pepper

Directions:
1. In a small bowl, stir together the tofu, horseradish, scallions, parsley, and garlic until well mixed.
2. Season with salt and pepper.
3. Serve immediately.

Nutrition Info:
- Info Per Serving: Calories: 20 ; Fat: 0 g ;Saturated fat: 0 g ;Sodium: 50 mg

Chimichurri Rub

Servings: ½
Cooking Time: X
Ingredients:
- 2 tablespoons dried parsley
- 2 tablespoons dried basil
- 1 tablespoon hot paprika
- 1 tablespoon dried oregano
- 2 teaspoons garlic powder
- 1 teaspoon dried thyme
- 1 teaspoon onion powder
- ½ teaspoon freshly ground black pepper
- ¼ teaspoon sea salt
- Pinch red pepper flakes

Directions:
1. In a small bowl, whisk together the parsley, basil, paprika, oregano, garlic powder, thyme, onion powder, pepper, salt, and red pepper flakes until well blended.
2. Transfer to an airtight container to store.

Nutrition Info:
- Info Per Serving: Calories: 18 ; Fat: 0 g ;Saturated fat: 0 g ;Sodium: 90 mg
-

Tzatziki

Servings: 4
Cooking Time: X
Ingredients:
- 1¼ cups plain low-fat Greek yogurt
- 1 cucumber, peeled, seeded, and diced
- 2 tablespoons fresh lime juice
- ½ teaspoon grated fresh lime zest
- 2 cloves garlic, minced
- Pinch salt
- ⅛ teaspoon white pepper
- 1 tablespoon minced fresh dill
- 1 tablespoon minced fresh mint
- 2 teaspoons olive oil

Directions:
1. In a medium bowl, combine the yogurt, cucumber, lime juice, lime zest, garlic, salt, white pepper, dill, and mint.
2. Transfer the mixture to a serving bowl. Drizzle with the olive oil.
3. Serve immediately or store in an airtight glass container and refrigerate for up to 2 days

Nutrition Info:
- Info Per Serving: Calories: 100 ; Fat: 4 g ;Saturated fat: 1 g ;Sodium: 56 mg

Tasty Tomato Sauce

Servings: 5
Cooking Time: 5 Minutes
Ingredients:
- 6 tablespoons low-sodium ketchup
- 2 tablespoons minced garlic
- 1½ tablespoons honey
- 1 tablespoon vinegar
- ½ teaspoon freshly ground black pepper

Directions:
1. In a small bowl, mix the ketchup, garlic, honey, vinegar, and pepper until well blended. Use immediately.

Nutrition Info:
- Info Per Serving: Calories: 46 ; Fat: 0g ;Saturated fat: 0g ;Sodium: 5 mg

Tangy Soy Sauce

Servings: 5
Cooking Time: X
Ingredients:
- 2 tablespoons low-sodium soy sauce (or 1 tablespoon soy sauce)
- 1½ tablespoons honey
- 1 tablespoon white vinegar
- 1 tablespoon minced garlic
- 1 teaspoon peeled minced fresh ginger

Directions:

1. In a small bowl, mix the soy sauce, honey, vinegar, garlic, and ginger until well blended. Use immediately.
Nutrition Info:
- Info Per Serving: Calories: 26; Fat: 0 g ;Saturated fat: 0 g ;Sodium: 205 mg

Fresh Lime Salsa

Servings: 5
Cooking Time: X
Ingredients:
- 3 tomatoes, coarsely chopped
- ¼ cup chopped white onion
- ¼ cup chopped fresh cilantro
- 1 tablespoon minced garlic
- 1 tablespoon freshly squeezed lime juice
- Sea salt

Directions:
1. In a blender, place the tomatoes, onion, cilantro, garlic, and lime juice and blend until smooth. Season with salt and use immediately.
Nutrition Info:
- Info Per Serving: Calories: 20; Fat: 0 g ;Saturated fat: 0 g ;Sodium: 36 mg

Silken Fruited Tofu Cream

Servings: 4
Cooking Time: 15 Minutes
Ingredients:
- 1 cup silken tofu
- ⅓ cup fresh raspberries
- 2 tablespoons orange-pineapple juice
- 1 tablespoon fresh lemon juice
- ½ teaspoon vanilla extract
- ⅛ teaspoon ground cinnamon
- Pinch salt

Directions:
1. In a blender or food processor, combine the tofu, raspberries, orange-pineapple juice, lemon juice, vanilla, cinnamon, and salt. Blend or process until smooth.
2. You can use this cream immediately or store it in an airtight glass container in the refrigerator for up to 2 days.
Nutrition Info:
- Info Per Serving: Calories: 49 ; Fat: 2 g ;Saturated fat: 0 g ;Sodium: 23 mg

Simple Dijon And Honey Vinaigrette

Servings: ⅓
Cooking Time: X
Ingredients:
- 3 tablespoons olive oil
- 1½ tablespoons apple cider vinegar
- 1 tablespoon honey
- 2 teaspoons Dijon mustard

- Freshly ground black pepper

Directions:
1. In a small bowl, whisk together the oil, vinegar, honey, and mustard until emulsified.
2. Season with pepper and serve.
Nutrition Info:
- Info Per Serving: Calories: 145 ; Fat: 14 g ;Saturated fat: 2 g ;Sodium: 38 mg

Sun-dried Tomato And Kalamata Olive Tapenade

Servings: 1¼
Cooking Time: X
Ingredients:
- ½ cup chopped sun-dried tomatoes
- ½ cup packed fresh basil leaves
- ¼ cup sliced Kalamata olives
- ¼ cup Parmesan cheese
- 2 garlic cloves
- 1 tablespoon olive oil
- Sea salt
- Freshly ground black pepper

Directions:
1. In a food processor or blender, place the sun-dried tomatoes, basil, olives, Parmesan cheese, garlic, and olive oil and pulse until smooth.
2. Season with salt and pepper.
Nutrition Info:
- Info Per Serving: Calories: 57 ; Fat: 3 g ;Saturated fat: 1 g ;Sodium: 207 mg

Cheesy Spinach Dip

Servings: 1½
Cooking Time: 25 Minutes
Ingredients:
- 1 cup thawed chopped frozen spinach
- ½ cup fat-free cottage cheese
- 2 tablespoons chopped sweet onion
- ¼ cup grated Parmesan cheese
- 1 teaspoon minced garlic
- Sea salt
- Freshly ground black pepper

Directions:
1. In a medium bowl, stir together the spinach, cottage cheese, onion, Parmesan cheese, and garlic until well combined.
2. Season with salt and pepper.
3. Place the dip, covered, in the refrigerator until you are ready to serve it.
4. Serve with vegetables or pita bread.
Nutrition Info:
- Info Per Serving: Calories: 79 ; Fat: 2 g ;Saturated fat: 1 g ;Sodium: 213 mg

Sweet Salad Dressing

Servings: 5
Cooking Time: X
Ingredients:
- ¼ cup low-sodium Worcestershire sauce (or ¼ cup Worcestershire sauce)
- 2 tablespoons minced garlic
- 1½ tablespoons honey
- 2 teaspoons onion powder
- ½ teaspoon freshly ground black pepper

Directions:
1. In a small bowl, mix the Worcestershire sauce, garlic, honey, onion powder, and pepper until well blended. Use immediately.

Nutrition Info:
- Info Per Serving: Calories: 39 ; Fat: 0g ;Saturated fat: 0g ;Sodium: 136mg

Lemon-cilantro Vinaigrette

Servings: ⅓
Cooking Time: X
Ingredients:
- 2 tablespoons freshly squeezed lemon juice
- 2 tablespoons chopped fresh cilantro
- 2 tablespoons chopped jalapeño pepper
- 1 teaspoon honey
- ½ teaspoon minced garlic
- Pinch sea salt
- Pinch freshly ground black pepper
- Pinch cayenne pepper
- ¼ cup olive oil

Directions:
1. In a blender, add the lemon juice, cilantro, jalapeños, honey, garlic, salt, pepper, and cayenne and pulse until very smooth.
2. Turn the blender on and pour in the olive oil in a thin stream.

Nutrition Info:
- Info Per Serving: Calories: 117 ; Fat: 13 g ;Saturated fat: 2 g ;Sodium: 60 mg

Spicy Honey Sauce

Servings: 5
Cooking Time: X
Ingredients:
- 2 tablespoons vegetable oil
- 1½ tablespoons honey
- 1 tablespoon minced garlic
- 1 tablespoon chili powder
- ½ teaspoon salt

Directions:
1. In a small bowl, mix the vegetable oil, honey, garlic, chili powder, and salt until well blended. Use immediately.

Nutrition Info:
- Info Per Serving: Calories: 78 ; Fat: 6 g ;Saturated fat: 0 g ;Sodium: 279 mg

Lemon-garlic Sauce

Servings: 5
Cooking Time: X
Ingredients:
- ¼ cup freshly squeezed lemon juice
- 2 tablespoons olive oil
- 1 tablespoon minced garlic
- 1 tablespoon dried oregano
- ½ teaspoon salt

Directions:
1. In a small bowl, mix the lemon juice, olive oil, garlic, oregano, and salt until well blended. Use immediately.

Nutrition Info:
- Info Per Serving: Calories: 55 ; Fat: 5 g ;Saturated fat: 1 g ;Sodium: 233 mg

Classic Italian Tomato Sauce

Servings: 4
Cooking Time: 20 Minutes
Ingredients:
- 2 teaspoons olive oil
- 1 onion, chopped
- 3 cloves garlic, minced
- 1½ pounds plum (Roma) tomatoes, chopped
- 2 tablespoons no-salt-added tomato paste
- 2 tablespoons finely grated carrot
- 1 teaspoon dried basil leaves
- ½ teaspoon dried oregano
- ⅛ teaspoon white pepper
- Pinch salt
- Pinch sugar
- 2 tablespoons fresh basil leaves, chopped

Directions:
1. In a large saucepan, heat the olive oil over medium heat.
2. Add the onion and garlic, and cook and stir for 3 minutes or until the onions are translucent.
3. Add the tomatoes, tomato paste, carrot, basil, oregano, white pepper, salt, and sugar, and stir and bring to a simmer.
4. Simmer for 15 to 18 minutes, stirring frequently, or until the sauce thickens slightly.
5. Stir in the fresh basil and serve.

Nutrition Info:
- Info Per Serving: Calories: 73 ; Fat: 3 g ;Saturated fat: 0 g ;Sodium: 19 mg

Double Tomato Sauce

Servings: 3
Cooking Time: 35 Minutes
Ingredients:

- 1 teaspoon olive oil
- ½ sweet onion, chopped
- 2 teaspoons minced garlic
- 1 (28-ounce) can low-sodium diced tomatoes with their juices
- ½ cup chopped sun-dried tomatoes
- Pinch red pepper flakes
- 2 tablespoons chopped fresh basil
- 2 tablespoons chopped fresh parsley
- Sea salt
- Freshly ground black pepper
- Whole-grain pasta or zucchini noodles, for serving (optional)

Directions:

1. In a large saucepan, warm the olive oil over medium-high heat.
2. Add the onions and garlic and sauté until softened, about 3 minutes.
3. Stir in the tomatoes, sun-dried tomatoes, and red pepper flakes and bring the sauce to a simmer.
4. Reduce the heat and simmer for 20 to 25 minutes.
5. Stir in the basil and parsley and simmer for 5 more minutes.
6. Season with salt and pepper.
7. Serve over whole-grain pasta or zucchini noodles.

Nutrition Info:

- Info Per Serving: Calories:94 ; Fat: 1 g ;Saturated fat: 0 g ;Sodium: 243mg

Mustard Berry Vinaigrette

Servings: 8
Cooking Time: 10 Minutes
Ingredients:

- 3 tablespoons low-sodium yellow mustard
- ½ cup fresh raspberries
- ½ cup sliced fresh strawberries
- 2 tablespoons raspberry vinegar
- 2 teaspoons agave nectar
- Pinch salt

Directions:

1. In a blender or food processor, combine the mustard, raspberries, strawberries, raspberry vinegar, agave nectar, and salt, and blend or process until smooth. You can also combine the ingredients in a bowl and mash them with the back of a fork.
2. Store the vinaigrette in an airtight glass container in the refrigerator for up to 3 days.

Nutrition Info:

- Info Per Serving: Calories: 27 ; Fat: 1 g ;Saturated fat: 0 g ;Sodium: 65 mg

Green Sauce

Servings: 4
Cooking Time: 15 Minutes
Ingredients:

- 1 cup watercress
- ½ cup frozen baby peas, thawed
- ¼ cup chopped fresh cilantro leaves
- 2 scallions, chopped
- 3 tablespoons silken tofu
- 2 tablespoons fresh lime juice
- 1 tablespoon green olive slices
- 1 teaspoon grated fresh lime zest
- Pinch salt
- Pinch white pepper

Directions:

1. In a food processor or blender, combine the watercress, peas, cilantro, scallions, tofu, lime juice, olives, lime zest, salt, and white pepper, and process or blend until smooth.
2. This sauce can be used immediately, or you can store it in an airtight glass container in the refrigerator up to four days.

Nutrition Info:

- Info Per Serving: Calories: 27 ; Fat: 1 g ;Saturated fat: 0 g ;Sodium: 65 mg

Honey-garlic Sauce

Servings: 5
Cooking Time: X
Ingredients:

- 2 tablespoons low-sodium soy sauce (or 1 tablespoon soy sauce)
- 1½ tablespoons honey
- 1 tablespoon minced garlic
- 2 teaspoons sesame oil
- 1 teaspoon freshly ground black pepper

Directions:

1. In a small bowl, mix the soy sauce, honey, garlic, sesame oil, and pepper together until well blended and use immediately.

Nutrition Info:

- Info Per Serving: Calories: 42 ; Fat: 2g ;Saturated fat: 0g ;Sodium: 205mg

Oregano-thyme Sauce

Servings: 5
Cooking Time: X
Ingredients:
- 2 tablespoons balsamic vinegar
- 1 tablespoon dried oregano
- 1 tablespoon dried thyme
- 1 tablespoon minced garlic
- ½ teaspoon salt

Directions:
1. In a small bowl, mix the vinegar, oregano, thyme, garlic, and salt until well blended. Use immediately

Nutrition Info:
- Info Per Serving: Calories: 10 ; Fat: 0 g ;Saturated fat: 0 g ;Sodium: 235 mg

Desserts And Treats

Kiwifruit Tart

Servings: 2
Cooking Time: 35 Min
Ingredients:
- For the crust:
- ¼ cup digestive biscuits, crumbled
- 1 tsp plant-based butter, melted
- For the filling:
- 4 oz nonfat cream cheese, at room temperature
- ⅓ cup nonfat plain yoghurt, at room temperature
- 1 large free-range egg
- ⅓ cup kiwifruit, puréed
- 2 tbsp. granulated sugar
- ½ tsp vanilla extract

Directions:
1. To make the crust:
2. Heat the oven to 300°F gas mark
3. In a small-sized mixing bowl, add the biscuit crumbs and butter, mix until combined.
4. Evenly divide the biscuit mixture between 2 (6– 8-oz) ramekins. Press the crumbs into a thin layer at the bottom of each ramekin.
5. Place them in the oven and bake for 5 minutes. Remove from the oven and set aside.
6. To make the filling:
7. In a medium-sized mixing bowl, beat the cream cheese with a hand mixer for 1 minute until very smooth.
8. Add the plain yoghurt and the egg and continue to beat until well blended. Scrape down the sides of the bowl and add the kiwifruit purée, sugar, and vanilla extract. Beat until smooth.
9. Divide the filling into the ramekins and smooth the tops. Return them to the oven and bake for 30 minutes until the centres are just set.
10. Cool the cheesecakes for 30 minutes on a wire rack, then place them in the refrigerator for 4 hours or overnight to chill completely.
11. Serve cold.

Nutrition Info:
- Info Per Serving: Calories: 251 ; Fat: 7g ;Saturated fat: 2 g ;Sodium: 321 mg

Loco Pie Crust

Servings: 8
Cooking Time: X
Ingredients:
- ½ cup plus
- 1 tablespoon mayonnaise
- 3 tablespoons buttermilk
- 1 teaspoon vinegar
- 1½ cups flour

Directions:
1. In large bowl, combine mayonnaise, buttermilk, and vinegar and mix well. Add flour, stirring with a fork to form a ball. You may need to add more buttermilk or more flour to make a workable dough. Press dough into a ball, wrap in plastic wrap, and refrigerate for 1 hour.
2. When ready to bake, preheat oven to 400ºF. Roll out dough between two sheets of waxed paper. Remove top sheet and place crust in 9″ pie pan. Carefully ease off the top sheet of paper, then ease the crust into the pan and press to bottom and sides. Fold edges under and flute.
3. Either use as recipe directs, or bake for 5 minutes, then press crust down with fork if necessary. Bake for 5–8 minutes longer or until crust is light golden brown.

Nutrition Info:
- Info Per Serving: Calories:171.83; Fat: 7.35 g ;Saturated fat:1.18 g;Sodium: 65.46 mg

Sweetato Bundt Cake

Servings: 12
Cooking Time: 45 Min
Ingredients:

- Cooking spray
- ¾ cup sweet potato, cooked and mashed
- ½ cup almond milk
- ½ cup brown sugar
- ⅓ cup sunflower oil
- 2 large free-range eggs
- 1¾ cups whole-wheat flour
- ¾ cup quick oats
- 1½ tsp baking powder
- ¾ tsp baking soda
- ¼ tsp ground cinnamon
- ¼ tsp ground nutmeg
- ¼ tsp ground allspice
- ½ cup dark chocolate chips

Directions:

1. Preheat the oven to 350°F gas mark 4.
2. Coat a Bundt cake pan with cooking spray and set aside.
3. In a stand mixer, add the mashed sweet potato, almond milk, sugar, sunflower oil, and eggs, beat until well blended.
4. In a large-sized mixing bowl, add the flour, oats, baking powder, baking soda cinnamon, nutmeg, allspice, and dark chocolate chips, mix to combine.
5. With the stand mixer on low, add 1 soup spoonful at a time of the dry ingredients into the wet ingredients, beat until well combined.
6. Spoon the batter into the prepared Bundt cake pan. Bake for 45 minutes, or until the toothpick inserted comes out clean.
7. Serve or store in an airtight container to stay fresh.

Nutrition Info:

- Info Per Serving: Calories: 242 ; Fat: 10g ;Saturated fat: 3 g ;Sodium: 104 mg

Dried Fruit Rolls

Servings: 10
Cooking Time: 8 Hours
Ingredients:

- Parchment paper
- 2 cups apricot purée
- 1 cup unsweetened applesauce
- 1 tbsp. organic honey
- ¼ tsp ground cinnamon
- ⅛ tsp ground nutmeg
- ⅛ tsp ground ginger
- Pinch ground allspice

Directions:

1. Heat the oven to 150°F or lower.
2. Line a baking sheet with parchment paper and set aside.

3. In a medium-sized mixing bowl, add the apricot purée, unsweetened applesauce, honey, cinnamon, nutmeg, ginger, and allspice, whisk until well blended.
4. Spread the apricot mixture on the baking sheet as thinly as possible.
5. Place the baking sheet in the oven and bake for 8 hours until the mixture is completely dried and no longer tacky to the touch.
6. Remove the dried fruit leather from the oven and cut it into 10 strips and roll them up.

Nutrition Info:

- Info Per Serving: Calories: 33 ; Fat:0 g ;Saturated fat: 0 g ;Sodium: 3 mg

Peach Melba Frozen Yogurt Parfaits

Servings: 4
Cooking Time: 5 Minutes
Ingredients:

- 2 tablespoons slivered almonds
- 1 tablespoon brown sugar
- 2 peaches, peeled and chopped (see Ingredient Tip)
- 1 cup fresh raspberries
- 2 cups no-sugar-added vanilla frozen yogurt
- 2 tablespoons peach jam
- 2 tablespoons raspberry jam or preserves

Directions:

1. In a small nonstick skillet over medium heat, combine the almonds and brown sugar.
2. Cook, stirring frequently, until the sugar melts and coats the almonds, about 3 to 4 minutes. Remove from the heat and put the almonds on a plate to cool.
3. To make the parfaits: In four parfait or wine glasses, layer each with the peaches, raspberries, frozen yogurt, peach jam, and raspberry jam. Top each glass with the caramelized almonds.

Nutrition Info:

- Info Per Serving: Calories: 263 ; Fat: 5 g ;Saturated fat: 1 g ;Sodium: 91 mg

Almond Strawberry Parfaits

Servings: 4
Cooking Time: 5 Minutes
Ingredients:

- ¼ cup sliced almonds
- ½ cup low-fat ricotta cheese
- ½ cup plain nonfat Greek yogurt
- 3 tablespoons powdered sugar
- ½ teaspoon vanilla
- Pinch salt
- 2 cups sliced strawberries
- 2 tablespoons strawberry jam
- 1 tablespoon balsamic vinegar

Directions:

1. In a small saucepan on the stovetop or in a glass bowl in the toaster oven, toast the almonds over low heat until they are golden. Transfer to a plate and set aside.
2. In a small bowl, combine the ricotta, yogurt, powdered sugar, vanilla, and salt.
3. In a medium bowl, combine the sliced strawberries, jam, and balsamic vinegar, and mix gently.
4. Make the parfaits by layering the ricotta mixture and the strawberry mixture into 4 parfait or wine glasses. Top each glass with the toasted almonds, and serve. You can make this recipe ahead of time and chill it up to 3 hours.
Nutrition Info:
- Info Per Serving: Calories: 158 ; Fat: 6 g ;Saturated fat: 2 g ;Sodium: 62 mg

Fruit Yoghurt Parfait
Servings: 2
Cooking Time: 20 Min
Ingredients:
- 2 cups plain Greek yogurt
- 1 banana, sliced
- ½ cup strawberries, sliced
- ¼ cup almonds, chopped
- ¼ cup unsalted sunflower seeds, roasted
- 2 tbsp. organic honey
- 1 tbsp. chia seeds, for garnish
- 1 tbsp. small dark chocolate chips, for garnish
Directions:
1. Divide the yoghurt between two serving bowls.
2. Evenly divide the banana, strawberries, almonds, and roasted sunflower seeds between the bowls.
3. Drizzle each bowl with 1 tbsp. of honey and top them with chia seeds and chocolate chips.
4. Serve cold.
Nutrition Info:
- Info Per Serving: Calories: 394 ; Fat: 18 g ;Saturated fat: 2 g ;Sodium: 57 mg

Blueberry Cloud
Servings: 4
Cooking Time: X
Ingredients:
- 1 (0.25-ounce) envelope unflavored gelatin
- ¼ cup cold water
- ¼ cup orange juice
- 3 tablespoons sugar
- 1 cup blueberries
- 1 cup vanilla frozen yogurt
- 1 cup frozen non-fat whipped topping, thawed
Directions:
1. In microwave-safe glass measuring cup, combine gelatin with water; let stand for 5 minutes to let gelatin soften. Add orange juice and sugar. Microwave on high for 1–2 minutes, stirring twice during cooking time, until gelatin and sugar dissolve. Pour into blender or food processor.
2. Add berries; blend or process until smooth. Let stand until cool, about 20 minutes. Then add yogurt; process until smooth. Pour into medium bowl and fold in whipped topping. Spoon into serving dishes, cover, and freeze for at least 4 hours before serving.
Nutrition Info:
- Info Per Serving: Calories: 183.28; Fat:4.72 g ;Saturated fat: 3.37 g;Sodium: 49.08 mg

Luscious Mocha Mousse
Servings: X
Cooking Time: 10 Minutes
Ingredients:
- 4 ounces 70-percent dark chocolate, finely chopped
- ¾ cup unsweetened soy milk
- ½ teaspoon espresso powder
- ½ teaspoon pure vanilla extract
- Pinch sea salt
- 4 ounces silken tofu, drained well
Directions:
1. Place the chocolate in a medium bowl and set aside.
2. In a small saucepan, warm the soy milk, espresso powder, vanilla, and salt over medium-high heat.
3. Bring the mixture to a boil and then pour it over the chocolate. Let the mixture stand for 10 minutes, then whisk until the chocolate is completely melted and the mixture is blended.
4. Pour the chocolate mixture into a food processor or blender and add the tofu. Pulse until very smooth.
5. Spoon the mousse into two bowls and refrigerate until firm, about 2 hours.
6. Serve.
Nutrition Info:
- Info Per Serving: Calories: 441 ; Fat: 38 g ;Saturated fat: 21 g ;Sodium: 213 mg

Mango Walnut Upside-down Cake
Servings: 12
Cooking Time: X
Ingredients:
- 2 tablespoons plus
- ¼ cup butter, divided
- ¼ cup dark brown sugar
- ¼ teaspoon cardamom
- ½ teaspoon cinnamon
- 1 mango, peeled and sliced
- ¼ cup vegetable oil
- ½ cup sugar
- ½ cup brown sugar
- 2 egg whites
- 1 egg

- ¼ cup yogurt
- ¼ cup orange juice
- 1 teaspoon baking powder
- 1 teaspoon baking soda
- 1½ cups flour
- ½ cup whole-wheat flour

Directions:

1. Preheat oven to 350ºF. Spray a 12-cup Bundt pan with nonstick baking spray containing flour and set aside. In small microwave-safe bowl, combine 2 tablespoons butter with dark brown sugar. Microwave on high for 1 minute until butter melts; stir until smooth. Add cardamom and cinnamon.

2. Spoon this mixture into prepared pan. Arrange mango slices on top; set aside.

3. In large bowl, combine ¼ cup butter, oil, sugar, and brown sugar and beat until smooth. Add egg whites and egg and beat well. Add yogurt and orange juice, then baking powder, baking soda, flour, and whole-wheat flour. Beat for 1 minute.

4. Pour batter over mangoes in pan. Bake for 50–60 minutes or until a toothpick inserted in cake comes out clean. Let cool for 5 minutes, then invert onto serving tray. If any mango mixture remains in pan, spoon over cake. Let cool completely.

Nutrition Info:

- Info Per Serving: Calories:274.81 ; Fat: 11.11 g ;Saturated fat: 4.47 g;Sodium:200.85 mg

Apple-cinnamon Flatbread

Servings: 5

Cooking Time: 25 Minutes

Ingredients:

- Olive oil, for greasing the pan
- 1½ cups whole wheat or whole-grain self-rising flour
- 1 cup low-fat plain Greek yogurt
- 2 Envy apples, peeled, cored, and thinly sliced
- 2 teaspoons cinnamon
- 1½ tablespoons maple syrup

Directions:

1. Preheat the oven to 350°F. Line a baking sheet with parchment paper and lightly grease it with olive oil.

2. In a medium bowl, mix the flour and yogurt together until smooth, then knead the dough into a ball.

3. Lightly flour your work surface, transfer the dough to the floured surface, and press it into a flat 8-inch circle. Transfer the flattened dough to the prepared baking sheet.

4. In a small bowl, mix the apples and cinnamon until well combined.

5. Arrange the apple slices on the dough and bake until the flatbread is slightly brown on the edges, about 25 minutes.

6. Remove the flatbread from the oven and drizzle with the maple syrup. Enjoy immediately.

Nutrition Info:

- Info Per Serving: Calories: 213; Fat: 2 g ;Saturated fat: 1 g ;Sodium: 37 mg

Chocolate Granola Pie

Servings: 12

Cooking Time: X

Ingredients:

- 3 tablespoons butter or margarine
- 2 (1-ounce) squares unsweetened chocolate, chopped
- ¼ cup brown sugar
- ½ cup dark corn syrup
- 2 teaspoons vanilla
- 1 egg
- 3 egg whites
- 2 cups Cinnamon Granola
- 1 Loco Pie Crust , unbaked

Directions:

1. Preheat oven to 350ºF. In large saucepan, combine butter and chocolate. Melt over low heat, stirring frequently, until smooth. Remove from heat and add brown sugar, corn syrup, vanilla, egg, and egg whites and beat well until blended.

2. Stir in granola and pour into pie crust. Bake for 40–50 minutes or until filling is set and pie crust is deep golden brown. Let cool completely and serve.

Nutrition Info:

- Info Per Serving: Calories: 384.56; Fat:14.45 g ;Saturated fat:4.65 g;Sodium:137.51 mg

Cashew Butter Latte

Servings: 1

Cooking Time: 10 Min

Ingredients:

- ¼ cup unsalted cashew butter
- 1 tsp vanilla extract
- 1 tsp organic honey
- ½ tsp ground cinnamon, plus more if needed
- 1 cup unsweetened cashew milk, more if needed

Directions:

1. Add the espresso, cashew butter, vanilla extract, honey, and cinnamon into a medium-sized stockpot over medium heat, whisking occasionally until the cashew butter has melted.

2. Heat the cashew milk over low heat in a small-sized stockpot. When it is warm (not hot), whisk it vigorously by hand, or use a handheld beater, to make it foamy.

3. Pour the hot coffee mixture into a mug and top with the foamy milk.

Nutrition Info:

- Info Per Serving: Calories: 169 ; Fat: 3 g ;Saturated fat:2 g ;Sodium: 128 mg

Peach Oat Bake

Servings: 2
Cooking Time: 30 Minutes
Ingredients:
- 1 tablespoon olive oil, plus more for greasing the baking dish
- 2 peaches, cored and sliced
- 2 teaspoons cinnamon, divided
- ½ cup steel-cut oats
- ¼ cup chopped walnuts
- 2 teaspoons maple syrup

Directions:
1. Preheat the oven to 350°F. Lightly oil a 7-inch-square baking dish.
2. In a medium bowl, mix the peaches with 1 teaspoon of cinnamon.
3. Scatter the peaches in an even layer on the bottom of the prepared baking dish.
4. In a small bowl, stir together the oats, walnuts, maple syrup, the remaining cinnamon, and 1 tablespoon of olive oil.
5. Distribute the oat mixture evenly over the peaches and bake for 30 minutes until lightly golden. Serve immediately.

Nutrition Info:
- Info Per Serving: Calories: 394 ; Fat: 19 g ;Saturated fat: 2g ;Sodium: 1 mg

Dark Chocolate Meringues

Servings: 18
Cooking Time: 15 Minutes
Ingredients:
- 2 egg whites, at room temperature
- ⅓ cup granulated sugar
- 3 tablespoons confectioner's sugar
- ¼ cup cocoa powder
- Pinch salt
- ½ teaspoon vanilla extract
- ¼ cup mini semisweet chocolate chips

Directions:
1. Preheat the oven to 350°F. Line a baking sheet with parchment paper and set aside.
2. In a clean, dry medium bowl, place the egg whites. Put the bowl inside a larger bowl filled with very warm water and let stand for 5 minutes to warm up the egg whites.
3. Remove the medium bowl from the large bowl and carefully dry the outside.
4. In another medium bowl, sift together the granulated sugar, powdered sugar, cocoa powder, and salt.
5. Start beating the egg whites and gradually add the sugar mixture, beating constantly, until the mixture stands in peaks that droop when you pull up the turned-off beater.
6. Fold in the vanilla extract and the chocolate chips.
7. Drop by tablespoons onto the prepared baking sheet.

8. Bake for 13 to 15 minutes or until the meringues are set. Cool on the baking sheet for 5 minutes, then remove to a wire rack to completely cool. Store in layers separated by wax paper in an airtight container at room temperature up to 3 days.

Nutrition Info:
- Info Per Serving: Calories: 35 ; Fat: 1 g ;Saturated fat: 1 g ;Sodium: 9 mg

Green Grapes With Lemon Sorbet

Servings: 4
Cooking Time: X
Ingredients:
- 2 cups green grapes
- 2 tablespoons sugar
- ½ cup sweet white wine
- 1 teaspoon orange zest
- 2 cups lemon sorbet

Directions:
1. Wash grapes, dry, and cut in half. Sprinkle sugar over grapes and let stand for 5 minutes. Then add wine, stirring gently until sugar dissolves. Sprinkle with orange zest, cover, and refrigerate for 1 hour.
2. When ready to serve, stir grape mixture and serve over sorbet in sherbet glasses or goblets.

Nutrition Info:
- Info Per Serving: Calories: 233.90; Fat:1.61 g ;Saturated fat: 0.90 g;Sodium: 35.64 mg

Balsamic Strawberry Yogurt

Servings: 4
Cooking Time: X
Ingredients:
- 2 cups low-fat unsweetened plain yoghurt
- 1 tbsp. organic honey
- 2 cups strawberries
- 2 tbsp. balsamic vinegar
- 2 tbsp. unsalted walnuts, chopped

Directions:
1. In a small-sized mixing bowl, add the plain yoghurt and organic honey, mix to combine.
2. In another small-sized mixing bowl, add the strawberries and the balsamic vinegar. Use a fork to lightly mash the strawberries in the vinegar. Rest for a few minutes.
3. Serve the yoghurt topped with ½ cup balsamic strawberries and ½ tbsp. walnuts.

Nutrition Info:
- Info Per Serving: Calories: 127 ; Fat: 2 g ;Saturated fat: 1 g ;Sodium: 89 mg

Pumpkin Pie Pudding

Servings: 4
Cooking Time: 5 Minutes
Ingredients:

- 1 tablespoon gelatin
- ¼ cup water
- 1 (12-ounce) can low-fat evaporated milk
- ½ cup pumpkin puree
- 1 tablespoon maple syrup
- 2 teaspoons cinnamon

Directions:

1. In a small bowl, sprinkle the gelatin over the water and set aside for 10 minutes.
2. In a medium saucepan over medium heat, stir together the evaporated milk, pumpkin puree, maple syrup, and cinnamon. Heat for about 5 minutes, or until it begins to foam.
3. Remove the pumpkin mixture from the heat and stir in the gelatin water.
4. Pour the pumpkin pie pudding through a fine sieve into four small (½-cup) ramekins, cover with plastic wrap, and refrigerate for 2 hours. Serve chilled.

Nutrition Info:

- Info Per Serving: Calories: 116 ; Fat: 2 g ;Saturated fat: 1g ;Sodium: 112 mg

Chocolate And Date Cupcakes

Servings: 9
Cooking Time: 20 Minutes
Ingredients:

- Olive oil, for greasing the pan
- 1 cup pitted Medjool dates
- ½ cup water
- 1 cup nut butter (such as almond, cashew, or all-natural peanut butter)
- ¾ cup liquid egg whites
- 3 tablespoons cocoa
- 1 teaspoon baking soda

Directions:

1. Preheat the oven to 350°F. Lightly oil 9 cups in a muffin tin and set aside.
2. In a blender, place the dates and the water and blend until smooth.
3. Add the nut butter, egg whites, cocoa, and baking soda to the blender and pulse until the mixture is a consistent texture.
4. Evenly distribute the batter into the greased cups. Each cup should be three-quarters full.
5. Bake for 20 minutes and serve immediately.

Nutrition Info:

- Info Per Serving: Calories: 236 ; Fat: 16 g ;Saturated fat: 1g ;Sodium: 176mg

Oatmeal Brownies

Servings: 16
Cooking Time: X
Ingredients:

- ¼ cup prune puree
- ¼ cup finely chopped dates
- ½ cup all-purpose flour
- ½ cup ground oatmeal
- ½ cup cocoa powder
- ½ teaspoon baking soda
- ½ cup brown sugar
- ¼ cup sugar
- 1 egg
- 1 egg white
- ¼ cup chocolate yogurt
- 2 teaspoons vanilla
- 2 tablespoons butter or plant sterol margarine, melted
- ½ cup dark-chocolate chips

Directions:

1. Preheat oven to 350ºF. Spray an 8″ square baking pan with nonstick cooking spray containing flour and set aside.
2. In small bowl, combine prune puree and dates; mix well and set aside. In large bowl, combine flour, oatmeal, cocoa, baking soda, brown sugar, and sugar, and mix well.
3. Add egg, egg white, yogurt, vanilla, and butter to prune mixture and mix well. Add to flour mixture and stir just until blended. Spoon into prepared pan and smooth top. Bake for 22–30 minutes or until edges are set but the center is still slightly soft. Remove from oven and place on wire rack.
4. In microwave-safe bowl, place chocolate chips. Microwave on 50 percent power for 1 minute, then remove and stir. Microwave for 30 seconds longer, then stir. If necessary, repeat microwave process until chips are melted. Pour over warm brownies and gently spread to cover. Let cool completely and cut into bars.

Nutrition Info:

- Info Per Serving: Calories:153.83; Fat: 4.88 g ;Saturated fat:2.63 g;Sodium:63.58 mg

Double Chocolate Cinnamon Nice Cream

Servings: 4
Cooking Time: 5 Minutes
Ingredients:

- 3 tablespoons semisweet chocolate chips
- 2 frozen bananas, cut into chunks
- ⅓ cup frozen mango cubes
- 2 Medjool dates, pit removed and chopped (see Ingredient Tip)
- 2 tablespoons flax or soy milk
- 3 tablespoons cocoa powder
- ½ teaspoon vanilla extract

- ½ teaspoon ground cinnamon
- Pinch salt

Directions:

1. In a small saucepan over low heat, melt the semisweet chocolate chips, stirring frequently. Transfer the melted chocolate from the pan to a small bowl to cool, and place it in the refrigerator while you prepare the rest of the ingredients. (Make sure to not let the chocolate harden.)

2. In a blender or food processor, combine the bananas, mangoes, dates, and milk and blend until well combined.

3. Add the cocoa powder, vanilla, cinnamon, salt, and the melted, cooled chocolate. Blend until the mixture is smooth.

4. This treat can be served right away or frozen for 2 to 3 hours before serving.

Nutrition Info:

- Info Per Serving: Calories: 221 ; Fat: 5 g ;Saturated fat: 4 g ;Sodium: 8 mg

Chocolate, Peanut Butter, And Banana Ice Cream

Servings: 2
Cooking Time: X

Ingredients:

- 2 frozen bananas, peeled and sliced
- 2 tablespoons cocoa powder
- 1 tablespoon honey
- 2 tablespoons all-natural peanut butter
- 1 tablespoon chopped walnuts (or nut of choice)

Directions:

1. Put the frozen bananas, cocoa powder, honey, and peanut butter into a high-speed blender and blend until smooth.

2. Transfer the ice cream mixture into a resealable container and freeze for 2 hours.

3. Once frozen, scoop the ice cream into two serving bowls and top with walnuts.

Nutrition Info:

- Info Per Serving: Calories: 269 ; Fat: 12 g ;Saturated fat: 2 g ;Sodium: 5 mg

Butterscotch Meringues

Servings: 30
Cooking Time: X

Ingredients:

- 3 egg whites Pinch of salt
- ¼ teaspoon cream of tartar
- 2/3 cup sugar
- 2 tablespoons brown sugar
- 10 round hard butterscotch candies, finely crushed

Directions:

1. Preheat oven to 250ºF. In large bowl, beat egg whites with salt and cream of tartar until foamy. Gradually beat in

sugar and brown sugar until stiff peaks form and sugar is dissolved. Fold in the finely crushed candies.

2. Drop by teaspoonfuls onto a baking sheet lined with aluminum foil or Silpat liners. Bake for 50–60 minutes or until meringues are set and crisp and very light golden brown. Cool on the cookie sheets for 3 minutes, then carefully peel off the foil and place on wire racks to cool.

Nutrition Info:

- Info Per Serving: Calories:29.39; Fat:0.06 g ;Saturated fat:0.04 g;Sodium: 17.97 mg

Chocolate Mousse Banana Meringue Pie

Servings: 8
Cooking Time: X

Ingredients:

- 1 recipe meringue pie shell
- 3 tablespoons cocoa powder
- 1 recipe Silken Chocolate Mousse
- 2 bananas, sliced
- 1 tablespoon lemon juice

Directions:

1. Follow directions to make meringue pie shell, but also beat cocoa into egg whites along with the sugar. Bake as directed in recipe. Let cool completely.

2. Make mousse as directed and chill in bowl for 4–6 hours until firm. Slice bananas, sprinkling lemon juice over slices as you work.

3. Layer mousse and sliced bananas in pie shell, beginning and ending with mousse. Cover and chill for 2–3 hours before serving.

Nutrition Info:

- Info Per Serving: Calories: 253.53; Fat:9.23 g ;Saturated fat: 5.94 g;Sodium:79.66 mg

Lemon Mousse

Servings: 4
Cooking Time: X

Ingredients:

- 1 (0.25-ounce) envelope unflavored gelatin
- ¼ cup cold water
- 1/3 cup lemon juice
- 2/3 cup pear nectar
- ¼ cup sugar, divided
- 1 teaspoon grated lemon zest
- 1 cup lemon yogurt
- 2 pasteurized egg whites
- ¼ teaspoon cream of tartar

Directions:

1. In microwave-safe glass measuring cup, combine gelatin and cold water; let stand for 5 minutes to soften gelatin. Stir in lemon juice, pear nectar, and 2 tablespoons sugar. Microwave on high for 1–2 minutes, stirring twice

during cooking time, until sugar and gelatin completely dissolve; stir in lemon zest. Let cool for 30 minutes.

2. When gelatin mixture is cool to the touch, blend in the lemon yogurt. Then, in medium bowl, combine egg whites with cream of tartar; beat until soft peaks form. Gradually stir in remaining 2 tablespoons sugar, beating until stiff peaks form.

3. Fold gelatin mixture into egg whites until combined. Pour into serving glasses or goblets, cover, and chill until firm, about 4–6 hours.

Nutrition Info:

• Info Per Serving: Calories: 151.27; Fat: 0.65 g ;Saturated fat: 0.40 g;Sodium:65.70 mg

Spicy Tofu Pudding

Servings: 5

Cooking Time: X

Ingredients:

• 1 (3.5 oz) 80% dark chocolate, roughly chopped

• 1 (14 oz) extra-firm tofu, water drained, and tofu patted dry

• 1 tsp vanilla extract

• 1 tsp organic honey

• 1 tsp ground cinnamon

• ¼ tsp cayenne pepper (optional)

Directions:

1. In a medium microwave-safe bowl, heat the chocolate pieces in the microwave for 2 minutes, in 30-second increments until they have melted.

2. In a food processor, add the tofu, vanilla extract, honey, cinnamon, cayenne pepper (if using), and the melted chocolate, blend for 1 minute until smooth, scraping down the sides as needed. Serve as is.

Nutrition Info:

• Info Per Serving: Calories: 131 ; Fat: 18 g ;Saturated fat: 4 g ;Sodium: 11 mg

Strawberry-rhubarb Parfait

Servings: 6

Cooking Time: X

Ingredients:

• 2 stalks rhubarb, sliced

• ½ cup apple juice

• 1/3 cup sugar

• 1 (10-ounce) package frozen strawberries

• 3 cups frozen vanilla yogurt

Directions:

1. In medium saucepan, combine rhubarb, apple juice, and sugar. Bring to a simmer, then reduce heat and simmer for 8–10 minutes or until rhubarb is soft.

2. Remove pan from heat and immediately stir in frozen strawberries, stirring to break up strawberries. Let stand until cool, about 30 minutes.

3. Layer rhubarb mixture and frozen yogurt in parfait glasses or goblets, starting and ending with rhubarb mixture. Cover and freeze until firm, about 8 hours.

Nutrition Info:

• Info Per Serving: Calories:210.56; Fat: 4.16 g ;Saturated fat: 2.48 g;Sodium: 64.41 mg

Blueberry Crumble

Servings: 5

Cooking Time: 20 Minutes

Ingredients:

• 3 tablespoons olive oil, plus extra for greasing the baking pan

• ½ cup chopped walnuts

• 1 cup pitted Medjool dates

• 1 cup steel-cut oats

• 1½ cups blueberries

• 1½ tablespoons honey

Directions:

1. Preheat the oven to 350°F. Lightly oil an 8-inch-square baking pan.

2. In a food processor or blender, pulse the walnuts until they are finely ground. Transfer to a medium bowl and set aside.

3. Place the dates in the food processor and pulse until they become a coarse paste. Transfer to the bowl and mix with the walnuts.

4. Add the oats and the olive oil to the bowl and mix until the mixture sticks together.

5. Press half of the oat mixture into the bottom of the prepared baking pan.

6. Spread the blueberries evenly over the oat mixture and drizzle with the honey. Top with the remaining half of the oat mixture.

7. Bake for 20 minutes until the berries are bubbly. Enjoy immediately.

Nutrition Info:

• Info Per Serving: Calories:375 ; Fat: 17 g ;Saturated fat: 2g ;Sodium: 2 mg

Dark Chocolate Brownie Bites

Servings: 12
Cooking Time: 18 Minutes
Ingredients:

- ¼ cup salted butter, melted
- ¼ cup puréed beets
- ½ cup packed brown sugar
- 3 tablespoons honey
- 1 teaspoon vanilla extract
- 1 egg
- 1 egg white
- Pinch salt
- ¼ teaspoon baking powder
- ½ cup whole-wheat flour
- ¼ cup all-purpose flour
- ⅓ cup cocoa powder

Directions:

1. Preheat the oven to 350°F. Line 24 mini muffin cups with mini paper liners and set aside.
2. In a medium bowl, combine the butter, beets, brown sugar, honey, and vanilla and mix well.
3. Add the egg and the egg white and beat until smooth.
4. In a separate medium bowl, combine the salt, baking powder, whole-wheat flour, all-purpose flour, and cocoa powder. Stir the dry ingredients into the butter-sugar mixture just until combined.
5. Spoon the batter among the prepared muffin cups, filling each about ⅔ full. Each cup should take about 1 tablespoon of batter.
6. Bake for 16 to 18 minutes or until the little brownies are set; they will have a shiny crust. A toothpick inserted into the center will come out with moist crumbs attached. Don't overbake them or they will be hard.
7. Let the brownie bites cool for 5 minutes, then remove them to a cooling rack. You can eat these warm or cool. Store in an airtight container at room temperature up to 3 days.

Nutrition Info:

- Info Per Serving: Calories: 141 ; Fat: 5 g ;Saturated fat: 2 g ;Sodium: 51 mg

Silken Chocolate Mousse

Servings: 6
Cooking Time: X
Ingredients:

- 2 (1-ounce) squares unsweetened chocolate
- 2 tablespoons butter
- ½ cup sugar
- 1 teaspoon vanilla
- ½ cup satin or silken soft tofu
- 1 cup chocolate frozen yogurt
- 1 cup frozen non-dairy whipped topping, thawed

Directions:

1. Chop chocolate and place in small microwave-safe bowl with the butter. Microwave on medium for 2–4 minutes, stirring twice during cooking time, until chocolate is melted and mixture is smooth. Stir in sugar until sugar dissolves.
2. In blender or food processor, place chocolate mixture and add vanilla and tofu. Blend or process until smooth. If necessary, let cool for 10–15 minutes or until lukewarm.
3. Then add the frozen yogurt and blend or process until smooth. Finally add the whipped topping and blend or process until just mixed. Spoon into serving glasses, cover, and chill for 4–6 hours before serving.

Nutrition Info:

- Info Per Serving: Calories: 219.73; Fat:12.12 g ;Saturated fat: 7.86 g;Sodium:78.14 mg

30 day meal plan

Day 1
Breakfast: Orange-vanilla Smoothie 14
Lunch: Spinach Artichoke Pizza 17
Dinner: Rice-and-vegetable Casserole 52

Day 2
Breakfast: Cinnamon Granola 14
Lunch: Cold Chicken With Cherry Tomato Sauce 23
Dinner: Corn-and-chili Pancakes 52

Day 3
Breakfast: Cranberry-cornmeal Muffins 14
Lunch: Cohawaiian Pizza 19
Dinner: Chicken Breasts With Salsa 23

Day 4
Breakfast: Raisin-cinnamon Oatmeal Bread 14
Lunch: Moroccan Chicken 23
Dinner: Salmon With Mustard And Orange 47

Day 5
Breakfast: Dark-chocolate Orange Scones 15
Lunch: Wasabi-roasted Filet Mignon 33
Dinner: Mixed Berry Chicken Salad 26

Day 6
Breakfast: Honey Rice Pudding 16
Lunch: Beef And Broccoli 33
Dinner: Florentine Quinoa Casserole 53

Day 7
Breakfast: Italian Baked Omelet 16
Lunch: Pineapple Curried Chicken 24
Dinner: Ratatouille 53

Day 8
Breakfast: Whole-grain Pizza Crust 16
Lunch: Spicy Rib Eye In Red Sauce 34
Dinner: Broiled Swordfish 47

Day 9
Breakfast: Apple-cinnamon Smoothie 16
Lunch: Risotto With Ham And Pineapple 34
Dinner: Kidney Bean Stew 53

Day 10
Breakfast: French Toast With Citrus Compote 17
Lunch: Lemon Tarragon Turkey Medallions 24
Dinner: Chili-sautéed Tofu With Almonds 54

Day 11
Breakfast: Buckwheat Pancakes 17
Lunch: Dark Beer Beef Chili 34
Dinner: Halibut Burgers 46

Day 12
Breakfast: Whole-grain Oatmeal Bread 18
Lunch: Fruit-stuffed Pork Tenderloin 35
Dinner: Salad Sandwich 54

Day 13
Breakfast: Cashew & Berry Shake 18
Lunch: Turkey With Prunes 25
Dinner: Crisp Polenta With Tomato Sauce 55

Day 14
Breakfast: Protein Cereal 18
Lunch: Canadian-bacon Risotto 35
Dinner: Red Snapper With Fruit Salsa 45

Day 15
Breakfast: Crisp Polenta Open-faced Sandwiches 19
Lunch: Herb-crusted Pork Tenderloin 35
Dinner: Spicy Catfish Tacos 44

Day 16
Breakfast: Egg White And Avocado Breakfast Wrap 19
Lunch: Piña Colada Chicken 25
Dinner: Spinach And Kale Salad With Spicy Pork 36

Day 17

Breakfast: Cowheat-bread Tuna Melt 19
Lunch: Beef Risotto 36
Dinner: Scallops On Skewers With Tomatoes 44

Day 18

Breakfast: Nutty Oat Bars 20
Lunch: Maple-balsamic Pork Chops 36
Dinner: Tofu And Root Vegetable Curry 55

Day 19

Breakfast: Baked French Toast Strips With Mixed Berry Sauce 20
Lunch: Grilled Turkey And Veggie Kabobs 25
Dinner: Portobello Burgers 55

Day 20

Breakfast: Apple-cinnamon Quinoa 20
Lunch: Pork Scallops With Spinach 37
Dinner: Baked Halibut In Mustard Sauce 44

Day 21

Breakfast: Hearty-grain French Bread 21
Lunch: Pork Tenderloin With Apples 37
Dinner: Stuffed Mushrooms 56

Day 22

Breakfast: Open-faced Tomato-basil Sandwiches 21
Lunch: Balsamic Blueberry Chicken 26
Dinner: Quinoa-stuffed Peppers 56

Day 23

Breakfast: Pork-and-slaw Sandwiches 21
Lunch: Steak-and-pepper Kabobs 37
Dinner: Tuna Patties 43

Day 24

Breakfast: Scrambled Egg Tacos 22
Lunch: Sirloin Meatballs In Sauce 38
Dinner: Chickpeas In Lettuce Wraps 56

Day 25

Breakfast: Avocado And Kiwi Green Smoothies 22
Lunch: Mediterranean Patties 26
Dinner: Southwestern Millet-stuffed Tomatoes 57

Day 26

Breakfast: Cream-cheese Cinnamon Rolls 22
Lunch: Turkey Cutlets Florentine 27
Dinner: Shrimp Stir-fry

Day 27

Breakfast: Mini Turkey Meatloaves 24
Lunch: Beef And Avocado Quesadillas 38
Dinner: Quinoa Pepper Pilaf 58

Day 28

Breakfast: Turkey Oat Patties 27
Lunch: Stuffed Meatloaf 39
Dinner: Wild Rice & Lentils 58

Day 29

Breakfast: Citrus Cod Bake 43
Lunch: Hawaiian Chicken Stir-fry 28
Dinner: Sirloin Steak With Root Vegetables 33

Day 30

Breakfast: Pork Quesadillas 33
Lunch: Chile Pork With Soba Noodles 39
Dinner: Fennel-grilled Haddock 43

INDEX

French Toast With Citrus Compote 17
Fresh Lime Salsa 74
Fried Green Tomatoes 68
Fried Tomatoes With Goat Cheese 64
Fruit Yoghurt Parfait 79
Fruit-stuffed Pork Tenderloin 35

G

Greek Quesadillas 65
Green Grapes With Lemon Sorbet 81
Green Sauce 76
Grilled Turkey And Veggie Kabobs 25

H

Halibut Burgers 46
Hawaiian Chicken Stir-fry 28
Hazelnut-crusted Chicken Breasts 32
Healthy Paella 50
Hearty-grain French Bread 21
Herb-crusted Pork Tenderloin 35
Homestyle Bean Soup 60
Honey Rice Pudding 16
Honey-garlic Sauce 76

I

Indian Vegetable Soup 67
Iron Packed Turkey 28
Italian Baked Omelet 16
Italian Chicken Bake 30

K

Kidney Bean Stew 53
Kiwifruit Tart 77

L

Lemon Mousse 83
Lemon Tarragon Turkey Medallions 24
Lemon-cilantro Vinaigrette 75
Lemon-garlic Sauce 75
Lemony Green Beans With Almonds 65
Lime Brussels Sprouts 66
Lime Turkey Skewers 31
Loco Pie Crust 77
Low-sodium Chicken Broth 69
Luscious Mocha Mousse 79

M

Mango Walnut Upside-down Cake 79
Mango, Peach, And Tomato Pico De Gallo 72
Maple-balsamic Pork Chops 36
Marinated Baby Artichokes 69
Mediterranean Patties 26
Mini Lasagna Cups 40
Mini Turkey Meatloaves 24
Mixed Berry Chicken Salad 26
Mixed Veg Salad 63
Moroccan Chicken 23
Mustard And Thyme–crusted Beef Tenderloin 41
Mustard Berry Vinaigrette 76
Mustard-roasted Almond Chicken Tenders 31

N

Nuts On The Go 64
Nutty Coconut Chicken With Fruit Sauce 28
Nutty Oat Bars 20

O

Oatmeal Brownies 82
One Pan Chicken 31
Open-faced Tomato-basil Sandwiches 21
Orange-vanilla Smoothie 14
Oregano-thyme Sauce 77

P

Peach Melba Frozen Yogurt Parfaits 78
Peach Oat Bake 81
Peanut-butter-banana Skewered Sammies 57
Piña Colada Chicken 25
Pineapple Curried Chicken 24
Pinto Bean Tortillas 55
Piri Piri Chicken 32
Pistachio-crusted Red Snapper 50
Poached Fish With Tomatoes And Capers 45
Pork Chops With Cabbage 40
Pork Loin With Cranberry Bbq Sauce 42
Pork Quesadillas 33
Pork Scallops With Spinach 37
Pork Tenderloin With Apples 37
Pork-and-slaw Sandwiches 21
Portobello Burgers 55
Potato Soufflé 58
Prosciutto Fruit Omelet 38
Protein Cereal 18
Pumpkin Pie Pudding 82

Made in the USA
Monee, IL
19 June 2023

36173673R00050